The Wake Up Call

Financial Inspiration Learned from 4:44 + A Step by Step Guide on How to Implement Each Financial Principle

By

Ash'Cash

DISCLAIMER

The advice contained in this material might not be suitable for everyone. The author designed the information to present his opinion about the subject matter. The reader must carefully investigate all aspects of any business decision before committing him or herself. The author obtained the information contained herein form sources he believes to be reliable and from his own personal experience, but he neither implies nor intends any guarantee of accuracy. The author is not in the business of giving legal, accounting, or any other type of professional advice. Should the reader need such advice, he or she must seek services from a competent professional. The author particularly disclaims any liability, loss, or risk taken by individuals who directly or indirectly act on the information contained herein. The author believes the advice presented here is sound, but readers cannot hold him responsible for either the actions they take or the risk taken by individuals who directly or indirectly act on the information contained herein.

Published by 1BrickPublishing
A division of Ash Cash Enterprises, LLC
Printed in the United States
Copyright © 2017 by Ash'Cash
ISBN 978-0983448686

DEDICATION

This book is dedicated to the lovers of sound who know that hip-hop is not just a music genre but a teaching tool and to those who are ready to use this tool to build their financial life the right way.

DEDICATION REQUEST

Please pass a copy of this book to anyone you care about and who is in need of some inspiration and motivation.

Table of Contents

Financial Freedom is Our Only Hope

"The burden of poverty isn't just that you don't always have the things you need, it's the feeling of being embarrassed every day of your life, and you'd do anything to lift that burden."

- JAY Z

Jay Z's 4:44 is the blueprint to bridging the wealth gap and solving economic inequalities for African Americans! Period!!!! After reading what many may think is a bold claim you either think I'm super on point or I'm crazy... (I don't think you can be in the middle on this one). Either way I think you should keep reading. To be frank, Jay-Z isn't saying anything that many have not said before, but this time it's different. Would you rather take relationship advice from your single aunt or from your 2nd cousin who's been married 40 years? Should you take money advice from your broke uncle or from Mr. Johnny who's had a successful business for years and can show you a thing a two about making money. Keep in mind I said "show you" and not "tell you"... Anybody can tell you anything but showing and proving is a little difficult. That's why Jay has the blueprint! He's not speaking in theory, he has actually cracked the code of economic acceleration for black and brown people and if we just take heed we can solve many of the injustices that exist today. I know it's a big claim but allow me to explain and I will have it all make sense.

At first, I was going to start this book with a history lesson on how African Americans have been disenfranchised by design and how slavery, Jim Crow Laws, lynching, The KKK, denial of voting rights, segregation (wait, maybe not segregation), redlining, and mass incarceration are all some of the reasons why African Americans rank dead last in creating generational wealth.

But why harp on the problem when there's a solution? Instead of luring you in with the facts, I might as well start with my opinion. Instead of telling you how African Americans spend close to $2 Trillion dollars a year on goods and services and really don't own anything, I can tell you how the financial lessons in 4:44 can help flip that 2 to a 4.... 4 to an 8... How the right assets can help your wealth appreciate (#Bars!).

When Jay says Financial Freedom is our only hope he is not exaggerating. Even before #45 took office we began to see a resurgence of racism. Mike Brown, Trayvon Martin, Philando Castile, Alton Sterling, Freddie Gray, Eric Garner, Sandra Bland, Kalief Browder and the countless other injustices are examples of what happens when our collective power is not respected. When there is no real consequence for injustice then we are simply begging for mercy, and no one respects a beggar! The truth of the matter is that money is power! Those who control the money, control everything else... Politics, Schools, Business, Police, Community and everything else in between.

Just to be clear racism isn't what the dictionary and the media want you to believe it is; which is defined as prejudice, discrimination, or antagonism directed against someone of a different race based on the belief that one's own race is superior. The true definition of racism (as stated by Dr. Claude Anderson in his powerful book #Powernomics) is when one group holds a disproportionate share of wealth and power over another group then uses those resources to marginalize, exploit, exclude and subordinate the weaker group. That's why when you turn on the television it seems like African-Americans are losing every-day! Because of systemic and institutionalized racism!

Without getting too deep into the history of black economics, we must realize that most Blacks have only been able to create 'real' wealth and financial freedom for the last 50 years – slavery lasted 223 years from 1640-1863, then reconstruction and Jim Crow laws lasted 102 years from 1863-1965. It wasn't until the post-civil rights era that we began to see the tides change. And to be clear most of this was LEGAL and sanctioned by the government. For a more in depth look at the government's involvement in wealth disparities and inequities please read "The Color of Law: A Forgotten History of How Our Government Segregated America" by Richard Rothstein.

I can go on and on about how we got here but 4:44 is the first step in making things right. A recent report titled "The Road to Zero Wealth," looks at the past 30 years of wealth accumulation across racial lines, as well as what the future will bring if current trends continue; it comes to the conclusion that by 2053, just 10 years after the country is projected to become majority non-white, black median families will own zero wealth and twenty years later, Latino median families will follow suit. White median families will continue to own six figures. The key words here are "If current trends continue!" That's why it's imperative that we get our collective economic lives together!

The following lessons in this book will give you a step by step guide on how to begin to create financial freedom for you, your family, and community. This is probably not the first or last time we will have this conversation and I can assure you that we have a steep mountain to climb, but if we all get on the same page then we can tip the scale and reach the mountain top faster.

You will learn about credit; what it is, how it works and how you can use it to build wealth. There is a step by step guide on how to buy real estate and the power it holds in the wealth creation process. We discuss appreciation and depreciation and how to spend your money wisely. We discuss starting a business, and creating multiple streams of income. We tackle spirituality and discuss how "This Spiritual S#@t Really Works" especially when it comes to your finances. You will learn about the importance of cooperative economics, how to pass down wealth to the next generation, and how to protect your ASSets through insurance, wills and trusts. This guide will give you the jump start needed to right the wrongs of economic inequality.

Without any further ado... The Wake Up Call: Financial Inspiration Learned from 4:44 + A Step by Step Guide on How to Implement Each Financial Principle.

CHAPTER 1:48

F%#K Living Rich and Dying Broke

"People look at you strange, say you changed.
Like you worked that hard to stay the same."

- JAY Z

Financial freedom our only hope, F*ck livin' rich and dyin' broke. A poignant line in the first released track, The Story of OJ, is a testament to some of his past decisions, where he reflects on money mistakes he has made, but also some of the mistakes we make as a community. Oftentimes our focus is on living for now and spending our income on things that bring instant gratification but when it's all said and done many of us aren't able to leave our children in a better financial position than how we arrived here. Using an example of an investment in artwork, that over time increased in value and triples its worth, is a classic example of what we call in the finance world, an appreciating asset. Here he is clearly illustrating that there's a right and wrong way to splurge. When we spend with no direction or goal we put our livelihood and those we are responsible for in jeopardy of continuing the cycle of poverty. With a few clever lines over a classic Nina Simone song Jay is simply telling us let's not live for now and realize that there may be more tomorrows not only for you but your family as well. Therefore, let's begin to invest our money in assets that can be passed down for generations to come.

I once read a story about a famous music exec and his interaction with a Jewish businessman. The story states that one day, the two had a conversation about culture and the Jewish man asked, "Do you know what my Jewish friends call the black community?" The exec said, "No, what do they call us?" He replied, "We call you liquid money. The same way that water falls out of a man's hands, money typically seeps out of a black person's hands the same way. Your community gets money and immediately gives it all away to people who aren't black. We see that as a huge business opportunity." They then continued to discuss how many black people on payday or when they get a lump sum of money (like a tax refund) will go to an Indian business to cash the check, an Asian beauty supply store, a corner store owned by Arabs and a department store owned by whites. The Jewish man continued to explain how, when it's all said and done, these other business people are waiting like hungry animals to devour Black people's money as if they are the prey.

Some may ask why it so important that money circulates within the same community? What does that do for the community? It shouldn't matter where you spend your money as long as you are getting the goods and services that you are looking for... Right? Wrong! The more money that comes into a community and is recycled within that community, the more opportunities that community can create for said community. Please keep in mind that I am not only talking about your physical community (Although it should start there.) You have your local community, The Hip-Hop or music Community, the Acting community, the sports community, the Afro-Tech community, the entrepreneurship community, and many more communities in which African-Americans participate in but have no real control (But this is changing).

The NFL, for example is 70% African-American (players that is), but has zero majority owners. With the controversy of Kolin Capernick not having a job simply because he took a non-violent stand (or knee) to call out the hypocrisy as it relates to the treatment of black and brown people in America; is a prime example of why ownership matters. Can you imagine if there were majority black owners in the NFL? Take it a step further... Imagine if many of our black millionaires and billionaires pooled their money together and started their own league? But I digress. The point is, there is power in numbers and despite what people want to make it seem like, black and brown people have the numbers and the power, if it is used the right way. What good is a light bulb in the dark if you don't turn on the switch? For the record, the NFL has Black part-owners like Venus and Serena Williams of the Miami Dolphins, Pastor Kirbyjohn Caldwell of the Houston, Texans and Reggie Fowler, who was a part-owner in the Minnesota Vikings, but no longer has stake in the team. As far as principle ownership in any sport goes, Michael Jordan of the Charlotte Bobcats is the only one. Again, how much more control and opportunities would African-Americans have if ownership was part of the mix and not just participation?

But let me take a step back for a second; Did you know that according to Maggie Anderson, author of "Our Black Year" "The lifespan of a dollar in the Asian community is 28 days, 19 days in the Jewish community, and approximately six hours in the African-American community! This is not a typo... ONLY SIX F#@King HOURS!!!! Often the argument is that not everything that one may need is provided by black owned businesses and that one shouldn't be relegated to buy a product or service just because it is owned by blacks. But according to a study done by the Kellogg School of Business, it doesn't take 100 percent of buying Black to make a dent in the Black community. The study states "that if the middle-class black consumers were to spend a little more with black firms and the mainstream firms that engage those black firms, there would be a creation of almost 1 million jobs that could benefit the black community." And when they say "a little more" they are just saying 7 percent more to be exact. Meaning an increase from the current spending of just 3 percent to 10 percent of their spending.

The simple truth is that in this place that we call America, home of the free and land of the brave, you have almost no power if you don't own anything, so in essence Freedom isn't free. Without ownership things can be taken away from you without notice. Instead of working for money we need to begin to allow our money to work for us. This means acting your wage and not your want size; using the income that you make to secure your true financial freedom. This begins with saving your money, using that money to create something that you own, make money from what you own, and repeat the cycle.

The first step in this process is to pay yourself first. Warren Buffett once said "Don't save what you have left after spending; spend what you have left after saving." This first powerful step will set you on the road to true financial freedom.

You may be at the crossroads right now as we speak. Telling yourself that the concept sounds good, it makes sense but right now you are in so much debt that you cannot afford to start saving or that your bills are too high or you don't make enough. Excuse my brashness but this is a lie! You must begin to save now, no matter what! It's time to create a new habit where proper financial management becomes automatic. If you do not begin the process of paying yourself before your bills you will forever keep the habit of being in debt or living paycheck to paycheck. Even if you are not living paycheck to paycheck and money is abundant right now, you still need to create this habit of changing your relationship with money so that your income isn't dependent on your physical labor. Making excuses is a habit too, so relinquish yourself from all of these negatives by taking action today. Again, excuse my brashness but this is not an option; you must begin today to invest in yourself! Anything else is unacceptable. The repercussions of not investing in yourself are severe and must be avoided at all cost.

Action: For any income you receive you must put away 10% into an account that is separate from the account you use to pay bills or conduct your daily transactions. These funds should not be easily accessible. My suggestion would be to open an account in a different financial institution from where you primarily bank so that you remove the temptation of spending this money; which we will now call your financial freedom fund (#FFF) or F@#K YOU FUND (#FYF) for those who have a boss that you can't wait to tell... Your #FFF or #FYF should consist of at least six to eight months of expenses. This will alleviate the stress and anxiety that most feel when an emergency happens. This ensures that if your source of income stops for whatever reasons you will be able to cover your expenses for at least 6-8 months as you work on establishing that source of income.

Once you have accumulated this amount, continue to save and the excess should be used to purchase income producing assets (We'll discuss this more in chapter 4). The best and most effective way to develop the habit of paying yourself first is to make it as painless as possible. You know the saying "out of sight, out of mind" if you make it automatic and make it invisible you will create the habit without it even disrupting your day to day life. If you work 9-5, arrange to have the money taken from your paycheck before you receive it, you'll never know its missing. If you work for yourself make sure that every time you get paid you are putting 10% aside for savings. If you get a steady amount, it's better to have automatic deductions come out of your bank account on a monthly basis. I suggest opening a no fee digital bank that is FDIC insured or a Credit Union.

Remember paying yourself first should be your first and most important bill that you pay every month. Doing it automatically alleviates the temptation of not saving at all... Paying yourself first is the first step needed to correct your finances and is intended to help those who are serious about gaining control over their financial situation. In order for this to work you must have discipline and invest in yourself. This will be the best investment you will ever make in your life!!

Forfeit the v12 Engine

*"Photoshoot fresh looking like wealth,
I'm about to call the paparazzi on myself."*

- JAY Z

As Jay-Z continues to reflect on his past spending decisions he states "I bought every V12 engine; I wish I could take it back to the beginning..." he is speaking specifically about the Porsche 911 Carrera ($91,000), the Ferrari F430 Spider ($112,000), the Rolls Royce Phantom ($417,825), the rare, Italian-built Pagani Zonda F ($670,000), The Bugatti Veyron Grand Sport ($2,000,000), The Maybach Exelero ($8,000,000), and countless other rare beauties that he has had the privilege of owning. One thing that Jay knows for sure is that no matter the price, cars decrease in value over time. Especially when he compares it to the real estate investment opportunities that he's missed. According to Jay, he could've bought a place in Dumbo before it was Dumbo for like $2 million, that same building today is worth $25 million; Guess how he's feeling? Dumbo!

While it seems like Jay is being a little tough on himself, especially since he's made many other smart investment decisions throughout his career, his point was received loud and clear. To be fair, he's told us about his love for the big-body Benzes, that dulls his senses way back in 2004 and since he hasn't seen the back of his eyelids since 96' it's safe to say that he can afford to live the life that he is living. When it comes to forfeiting the v12 engine; used here as a metaphor to say that we must, again, act our wage and live below our means, we are saying that in order to create true financial freedom the second step is to make wise decisions with how we spend our money. Financial Expert Lynn Richardson said it best, "Rich people stay rich because they act poor; while poor people stay poor because they act rich."

Some may read this as saying we must not buy the things we want in life but it's quite the opposite. In order to live a fulfilling life, it is important to live the life that we imagine, we just shouldn't do it at the expense of the things that matter most. For many of us, spending money freely comes down to a few things; one of them being lack. When we feel deprived or feel that we are lacking something in our lives the first thing we do when our situation changes is go overboard. Somehow in our subconscious we want to make up for lost time and "live it up" because "who knows what tomorrow will bring". Having a "live for today, because tomorrow's not promised" attitude can really set you back financially. Having money is one thing but being able to keep it, grow it, and spend it wisely is another. That's why we must create a roadmap for our money by way of budgeting.

Budgeting is about creating the habit of knowing what's coming in and controlling what goes out. It's about taking your finances seriously and being able to eliminate unexpected surprises. There are good expenses and bad ones, creating a budget is about identifying which is which. Now is the time to understand the difference between needs, wants, assets and liabilities. Instead of spending so much money on the things we want and not enough money on the things we need or spending money on liabilities then convincing ourselves that they're assets, we must put our money in its place.

Just to be clear, a "need" is something you must have in order to live and a "want" is something you like to have but CAN survive without. When creating your budget if you understand how to identify between the two, then it will become easier to find money to pay yourself first and take care of your responsibilities.

Assets and Liabilities are another grey area many people need help with clarifying. Simply put, assets are things that you OWN that have Value and can increase in value, or can be sold without losing any of your original investment. The preceding sentence is important to repeat to understand what an asset really is... "Assets are things that you own that have value and can increase in value, or can be sold without losing any of your original investment." There are some rare cases in which an asset can lose value but those are exceptions. The v12 engine with all of its bells, whistles, conveniences, and luxuries is absolutely NOT an asset! In fact, according to Edmunds.com your car on average will depreciate 20% as soon as you drive it off the lot. That means that the $100,000 car that you dream of buying using your hard earned $20,000 as a down payment will lose that same $20,000 in a matter of minutes. On the other hand, if you spent that same $20,000 as a down payment on an investment property that paid you $3,000 a month in rental income, then not only would you be adding an extra $36,000 a year to your income (minus the mortgage and any expenses you have to pay to maintain the property) but you would also keep all of your original investment and then some! The car in this example is your liability because not only do you lose money from depreciation but you also lose it from paying interest; if   you financed the car. The investment property is your asset; it is giving you income each month and on average your property will increase in value. This is a classic example of merrily merrily eating off of streams... multiple streams, which we call passive or residual income (I'll explain this in a later chapter).

Not knowing how to create a budget or believing that a budget is too difficult to put together are two of the main reasons why people don't do it in the first place. Creating a budget is usually associated with being a complicated task that is time consuming with many numbers to calculate. Contrary to popular belief, creating a budget is a very easy task that most can start immediately. If you are creating a budget for the first time, you need to take a month to create a spending diary which is simply the process of you recording on a daily basis where your money is currently going. You can use a small composition notebook or visit www.IamAshCash.com/forms to download one for free. A spending diary is important so that you understand where your money leaks are and it gives you an opportunity to fix them with your first budget. Once you begin your budget you should update it monthly or as needed. Keep in mind that even if you are currently meeting all your monthly obligations comfortably you should still create a budget; wasting money is wasting money, whether you are in the red (deficit) or in the black (surplus). Having a budget creates structure and discipline, which is why you should start immediately.

Before you begin the process, there are a few things you must take into consideration. First, creating a budget is not a punishment, it is not meant to be difficult and it is not meant to complicate things. It is meant to free you of stress and give you balance and the freedom to do whatever you want, whenever you want to do it (within your means). Do not fool yourself! In order for your budget to really work, you must make sure it contains realistic goals that you can keep. If you love to go out drinking with friends and under entertainment you have $0, you are only fooling yourself. Maybe cut out the cable bill since you're really never home and put that money towards entertainment. The key is to be realistic.

Second, you must learn better ways to manage your money. Instead of taking constant trips to the local supermarket for your groceries and spend more money buying things with a markup, economize and shop at a discount warehouse like Costco's, BJ's or Sams' Club. Learn how to stretch your dollar.

Third, you have to make the commitment to follow your budget. Anyone can create one, but in order to have financial freedom you must create the habit of being responsible with your finances. This means that you have to follow your budget no matter what. Don't just create it one time and leave it, you must revisit it at least once a month to be successful.

The following are the steps that you need to take in order to create a successful budget:

Get it together: Step 1 is to get all of your important documents together. This should include all financial statements, investments, pay stubs, dividends, annuities, child support, alimony, everything! Anything you pay out each month and everything you receive as income! This will help you get organized in order to create the budget accurately and truly understand your bottom line.

Bottom Line = Income - Expenses

Show me what you got: Whether you're using the manual or electronic version of a budget, you must write down all the sources of income that you receive.

Give it to me: Write down all of your expenses in the expense column recording everything that has to be paid each month. First and foremost, recording your "pay yourself first" money. Then your mortgage or rent, car payment or transportation, insurance payments, food, utilities, entertainment, dry cleaning, laundry, etc;

Break it down: First break down your expenses into two categories; fixed and variable. Fixed expenses are expenses that don't change from month to month. Variable expenses are expenses that can vary depending on usage (make sure that you monitor your variable expenses so that they don't go over a certain amount each month).

Add it up: Total up all of your income and expenses making sure that expenses are not greater than income. If income is greater than expenses; congratulations you have a positive bottom line and more money to save. If expenses are greater than income than your bottom line is negative and you must make adjustments. There are only three ways that you can increase your bottom line.

1. Cut Expenses
2. Increase Income or
3. Do both!

To cut expenses; first try to minimize or limit things that are not a necessity (never adjust your "pay yourself first" money), For tips on increasing your income please visit *chapter 4.*

Check yourself: It is imperative that you review your budget monthly and make all the necessary adjustments as your life changes. It is irresponsible to think that your expenses are just going to remain the same from month to month. Keep a watchful eye and again stay honest!

Action: Using a blank piece of paper, begin to create your budget as instructed. (For a digital copy of a worksheet please visit *www.IamAshCash.com/forms*)

Your budget is your first practical tool that will determine how serious you are about living financially free! You can't get to a destination if you don't know where you're going! Stop living life blindly, open your eyes and begin to feel the joy of knowing that you're in control.

Credit... That's How They Did It

"Respect the game that should be it!
What you eat don't make me sh*t!"

- JAY Z

Now for the controversy... Jay-Z raps, "You wanna know what's more important than throwin' away money at a strip club?" he answers, "Credit." "You ever wonder why Jewish people own all the property in America? This how they did it." Some people have criticized Jay-Z saying that his line about Jewish people's property ownership was anti-Semitic. While there are long standing Jewish stereotypes about money and banking, including the accusation that world banking is dominated by the Rothschild family and that Jews control Wall Street and the United States Federal Reserve, Jay's implication and intent was far from trying to be hostile or prejudice towards Jews.

In his own words during a Rap Radar podcast interview, Jay-Z said "It's hard for me to take that serious because I exaggerated every black image in the world. Even you as the Jewish community, if you don't have a problem with the exaggeration of the guy eating watermelon and all the things that was happening, if you don't have a problem with that, and that's the only line you pick out then you are being a hypocrite. And I can't address that in a real way and gotta leave that where that is because it was exaggeration. Of course, I know Jewish people don't own all the property in America. I own things."

In all honestly it seems that Jay is attempting to draw a comparison between the struggles of African-Americans and Jews. Within the history of America and across the globe, both groups have been systematically marginalized and oppressed and despite that, both groups have been able to do some extraordinary things. In fact, Jay-Z is simply praising Jews for what they've been able to do, despite what they've gone through, and he is urging others (not only African-Americans) to do the same.

When you get past the controversy, credit is absolutely more important than the almighty strip club. In fact, it is one of the most important financial tools that can be used to grow someone's wealth; if you know how to use it right. Case in point: Jay-Z and Beyoncé recently used credit themselves to leverage their wealth in a real way. Even though they are worth more than a billion dollars combined, they took out a $52.8 million mortgage for their Bel-Air mansion. Using a blind trust (We'll talk about this in chapter 10) they paid $88million for their beautiful estate and financed the rest of the $135 million home. You may be asking why wouldn't they just pay cash for the whole home? Well with historically low mortgage rates, taking out a loan allows them to put their cash to better use. To drive the point home; let's say they are paying 4% on their $52.8 million mortgage, if they are able to invest that $52.8 million of their own cash in something that is paying 10% they are better off because the $528,000 they would make on the interest would easily pay the $211,000 interest payment from the mortgage; leaving them with a profit of $317,000 x 30 years = $9,510,000 which is the amount of money they made by using someone else's money… GENIUS!!!!

Whether we realize it or not, credit allows us to use other people's money to make our money work for us and that is the true definition of financial freedom. Many Americans struggle with credit but as a group, African-Americans have struggled the most. According to a 2010 U.S. Federal Reserve Bank report that surveyed the credit worthiness of home borrowers, all groups except for Black consumers had average credit scores above 700. Asian borrowers saw the highest average FICO score of 745, followed by Non-Hispanic Whites at 734, Hispanic whites at 701, All others at 732, and the average American scored 728. Blacks had an average of 677 which is considered fair. Add to that, many African-Americans are credit invisible which means they have insufficient credit histories to generate a credit score, and you can see why collectively we have to get our FICO act together.

Bad credit, low credit, and no credit not only stops you from making smart moves from a wealth building perspective but it also hurts your everyday life. Bad credit is expensive and will steal from your bottom line in ways you don't even realize. People believe that bad credit alleviates you from borrowing when it's quite the opposite. Bad credit is so lucrative that companies make trillions of dollars giving credit to those who have no or low credit scores. The next time you see an ad that says "No Credit, Low Credit, No problem" RUN!!!! They are not doing you any favors, they are literally stealing your money and you are allowing them. It's time to get smart about building your FICO score.

For those who are not familiar, FICO is a credit reporting system started by the Fair Isaacs Corporation. It is a numerical measurement of your credit worthiness that ranges from 300 to 850. Anything below 640 is bad credit or needs improvement, from 641-680 is fair credit, from 681-720 is good credit, and anything above 721 is excellent credit. Your FICO score is used by most lenders to determine whether or not you can obtain credit so using it the wrong way can be detrimental. Your score can stop you from getting loans, renting or buying a home, purchasing a car (even though we shouldn't be using credit for that), opening a bank account or even getting a job.

The concept of credit is simply "buy now, pay later" and it has been around for many, many years. In fact, some believe credit goes back more than three thousand years and started with the Egyptians and Babylonians. So, you can imagine that credit, as we know it today, has had many evolutions.

Believe it or not, not too long-ago credit information was gathered by the welcome wagon representative, who would judge you based on things like the quality of your home, your furniture, opinion of your character, etc. (Welcome wagon representatives were commercial greeters who would knock on a new neighbor's door to welcome them to the neighborhood.) Back then, if you applied for a loan, the lending decisions were made based on what was on your report, which was someone's flawed opinion, and on how the underwriter at the bank felt about you. Yup, their intuitive hunch! (Another flawed opinion.) If you didn't "look right" or if you were from some minority group or lived in the wrong neighborhood, then your chances of getting credit was slim to none.

Around the late 1960s, as credit became more popular, it was impossible for banks to personally interview all applicants or rely solely on the credit reports it was using. At the same time, congress had begun investigating discrimination cases that included housing loans and the practices of collection agents. More specifically, redlining which was a discriminatory practice where banks, insurance companies, etc., would refuse or limit loans, mortgages, insurance, etc., within specific geographic areas, especially inner-city neighborhoods. In fact, this practice is what gave whites a head start on wealth building through home ownership because minorities where literally unable to participate in the home buying process.

Because of this, we saw the birth of three federal regulations that would forever impact the credit game. In 1971, we were introduced to the Fair Credit Reporting Act (FCRA), which tried to make sure that your credit report was accurate, fair, and private. In 1975, we were introduced to the Fair Credit Billing Act (FCBA), which tried to protect consumers from unfair billing practices and to give us (consumers) a way to address billing errors in our revolving credit accounts. And, lastly, in

1977, we were introduced to the Fair Debt Collection Practices Act (FDCPA), which tried to eliminate abusive practices by debt collectors and aimed to make sure that what was on your credit report was correct. These three regulations forced the credit reporting agencies to act in a more fair, respectable, and responsible manner. But, of course, there were loopholes.

As the information in a person's credit report became more standardized, credit providers began to rely on them more than on the gut feeling of the underwriter. Lenders started to create their own automated risk-scoring systems, but because the results were inconsistent and inaccurate they continued to look for a system that was more reliable.

Enter Bill Fair and Earl Isaac, the founders of the Fair Isaac Company, which is better known as FICO. In 1956, they started FICO as a way to develop and market their credit scoring concept. In the early years, FICO marketed their scoring system to financial service companies that were trying to find a faster and more accurate way to make credit decisions.

The breakthrough came during the late 80s as computer software automation became popular with many businesses. In 1989, FICO introduced an automated credit scoring system that was marketed as "the impartial, consistent way to evaluate credit applications, taking the prejudice and instinct out of the equation." In layman's terms this was the most accurate, consistent, and fair way to judge someone's creditworthiness. Given that lenders were being put under pressure by congress to get rid of discriminatory lending practices, FICO seemed to be the answer to their problems and the system was quickly embraced by credit card companies and other credit issuers. This was the beginning of FICO's reign as the premier and universally accepted credit scoring system.

Then, in 1995, the deal was sealed when top mortgage issuers Fannie Mae and Freddie Mac stipulated that mortgage lenders incorporate FICO Score in their approval process. This is why today the FICO Score is THE most important score as it relates to your credit.

FICO isn't the only game in town though. In fact, on the market there are hundreds of other scores sold by the credit bureaus to lenders, insurance companies, credit card companies, landlords, finance companies, telephone companies, and any other entity that needs your information for sales or marketing purposes. There are scores that tell lenders who might be more likely to default on an existing mortgage, who should be offered lower interest rates, or who should have higher limits on their credit card. There are even global scores used by large corporations conducting business internationally.

In 2006, Vantage Score was created in collaboration with the three big credit bureaus—TransUnion, Equifax, and Experian—in a concerted effort to overtake FICO's lead in the market. Vantage Score became a new generic, but exclusive, credit score model marketed as a more "consistent interpretation" and "accurate score" than FICO. FICO responded to its competition in 2009 by creating the FICO® 8 Score, which touts that its new formula will significantly enhance the score's ability to predict consumer credit risk. This is important to know because when you use free services that give you your "credit score" please understand which score they are giving you.

Despite all of the competition and for now, the original FICO Score continues to be the clear leader and the score that matters most. It is a fact that most lenders, with a few exceptions, use FICO in making their credit decisions. (Some banks still do manual underwriting and most employ an internal risk calculation of which FICO is only a portion.)

Getting a handle on your FICO score is easy if you educate yourself on how FICO is calculated then discipline yourself to get it right. The five categories that are used to calculate your score are: amount of debt you have, payment history, debt usage ratio (how much you owe in relation to your credit limit), length of credit history and your mix of various types of credit

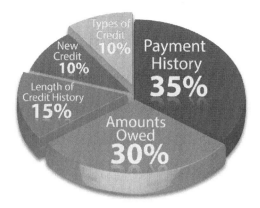

In order to get your credit back on track and keep it that way, there are five things you must avoid:

1) Do Not Make late payments

Obviously, we should know why this is a big no no but just in case here's why — credit is given based on your ability to pay back your obligations on time. Making late payments simply shows creditors that you are having a hard time meeting your obligations. Late payments stay on your credit report for up to seven years so it's imperative that you avoid them at all cost. If you've made some late payments in the past, it's not the end of the world. As you continue to make payments on time your previous late payments will have less of a negative impact. The key is discipline and showing creditors you are responsible.

2) Do Not Carry big balances

Most people don't realize this but creditors usually extend credit to those who they feel don't need it (like Jay-Z and Beyoncé) with the hopes that they'll use it eventually. Carrying a big balance shows creditors that you're having money issues and are relying too heavily on the credit to get you by. This has a negative effect on your credit score as well as with your ability to obtain new credit at a reasonable rate. As a rule of thumb, you should keep your usage down to about 30 percent (10% if you want a 700+ credit score); for example, if your credit card limit is $1,000 you should not carry a balance greater than $300

3) Do Not Close a Credit Line Unnecessarily

Closing a credit line can hurt you in two ways. It can increase your usage ratio because you no longer have that credit limit available to you; bringing your usage ratio over the recommended 30%. It can also affect you because it may eliminate a rich part of your credit history. If you have a card that has been open for a while and you've been making payments on time it is best to keep that line open. This allows future lenders to see your payment history. Most people close credit lines because they don't want to have too much credit available if they're not using the card or they may have received a new line with a better rate. In these instances, the best thing to do is to call your creditor and negotiate a lower rate or fees. Keep in mind that you lose more by closing your old lines.

4) Do not Have too many credit inquiries

Anytime a creditor checks your credit it affects your FICO score by at least 2 points. The deduction in points may only last for about six months but it is still important to use caution. Car dealers and mortgage brokers usually run your credit with multiple banks in an attempt to qualify you and get you the lowest rate; fortunately, if you are shopping for a car or mortgage within 45 days all of those inquiries will count as one.

5) Defaulting

Defaulting on any type of loan or credit card is the single worst thing you can do to your credit. Defaulting will surely get you declined for any new loans or have you paying more in interest than what you borrow. This should be avoided at all cost! If you ever foresee that you can't meet some or all of your obligations it is imperative that you reach out to your creditors as soon as possible. Most will be willing to work with you.

All in all, your FICO score can be manageable if you are proactive. Take care of any issues you foresee ahead of time and be disciplined about the way you use your credit. It is a best practice to understand your credit score and where you stand at all times. Certain states mandate by law to provide everyone a free copy of their credit report once a year from the three main credit bureaus which are Transunion, Equifax, and Experian. Please visit www.AnnualCreditReport.com to see if your state participates. You can also go to CreditKarma.com and open a free account to monitor your credit score. Also, check with your credit card company because many of them are now offering free credit monitoring tools. If you notice anything on your report that shouldn't be there, you should report it immediately.

If you are interested in a deeper dive into credit please pick up my best-selling book, What the FICO: 12 Steps to Repairing Your Credit (1Brick Publishing)

Merrily Merrily
Eat off these Streams
(Multiple Streams)

*"You can want success all you want, but to
get it, you can't falter. You can't slip, you can't
sleep. One eye open, for real, and forever."*

- JAY Z

I f there is any part of Jay's business acumen that I
appreciate the most it would be his ability to secure the
bag aka create multiple streams of income. When he
exclaims that he is "merily, merily, eating off these streams",
not only is this a play on his ability to profit off of his streaming
service Tidal, but also the fact that he has multiple businesses
that net him a profit. If Jay decided not to work another day in
his life, he would still be a very wealthy man. This is mainly true
because he has mastered the art of building wealth through
passive income (Even though he still chooses to keep some of
his income active).

Active income as defined by the IRS as income earned
through physical labor or income that you have to be physically
present to receive. Passive income on the other hand is defined
as income that the recipient does not have to physically work
for too obtain. For example, money earned from a business
that does not require the owner to be directly involved, rental
income, royalties from publishing intellectual property, money

earned from internet advertisements on a website you own, payments for a product or service that must be renewed on a regular basis in order to continue receiving its benefits, dividends and interest income from stocks and bonds, and money from a pension fund.

Until you own your own, you can't be free! In most cases it is difficult to create passive income without ownership. You have to own property, whether it is intellectual, physical, or real that has value to someone else in order to make your money work for you. Through Jay's ownership in music, spirits, clothing, sports, technology, and startups, he has created an empire that will continue to bear fruit for many years to come. This is a concept that most wealthy people have in common. Being rich is having money, being wealthy is having time. With two new additions to his family (S/O Sir and Rumi), time is definitely what he is after these days but his business decisions have been what has afforded him this luxury.

In order to build wealth, you must change your relationship with money. Don't look at money as something you have to work for; instead money should be something that works for you. Remove yourself as the employee of money and become the employer. By creating passive income, you remove the dependency on physical labor and free up more time for you to live stress free, doing what we want to do.

Making money work for you is an essential part of financial freedom. As long as you continue to keep your "work for money" mentality you will never be in control of your finances or your life. When the economy is doing badly and jobs are being cut, those who work for money are the ones who are affected the most. The people who have money work for them may be affected as well but on levels so small that it doesn't disrupt their day to day lifestyle. Creating passive income is the only way to alleviate the stress that comes with economic downturns.

If you weren't born into a wealthy family or weren't given an inheritance then obviously you have to accumulate money in order to make it work for you. There are many options to choose from when beginning to create passive income. The following are my top options:

CREATE INTELLECTUAL PROPERTY

Intellectual properties like books, eBooks, poetry, songs, movies, etc.; are great ways to bring you passive income by way of royalties. Some people make a career out of their intellectual property and some do it as a hobby. Either way taking it seriously and retaining your ownership rights can make this a very lucrative option.

In 1992 when the movie The Bodyguard was released starring Kevin Costner and Whitney Houston; the lead song for the movies soundtrack was "I will always love you" performed by Whitney Houston. This song was a smash hit; it spent fourteen weeks at the top of the U.S. Billboard 100 and sold a total of 42 million copies worldwide to date. Whitney received many accolades for the song and was the main reason why it did so well. She made a lot of money through royalties, but the true recipient of the riches and success went to none other than songwriter, actress and philanthropist miss Dolly Parton. Dolly wrote the song in 1974 and while everyone thought Whitney was the mastermind behind it, Dolly was home collecting millions of dollars for something she created close to twenty years ago.

START A BLOG, PODCAST OR VIDEO SERIES:

If you are particularly knowledgeable about a specific topic or subject then creating a blog, podcast or video series can create a source of passive income for you. Essentially you would write and/or talk about your topic or subject and as more people visit your site, you can begin earning income by placing ads on your blog, podcast or video series. This is a rather lucrative option but keep in mind, you get what you put in. If you are only producing content once in a while then expect the checks to come in once in a while. But if you are consistent then your audience will stick with you, tell their friends and family about you and ultimately gain you more eyeballs which equals to a bigger paycheck.

CREATE AN ONLINE COURSE

Similar to your blog, podcast, or video series; you can create passive income by creating an online course, teaching perspective students something you are an expert in. You can host your own online school using websites like Teachable.com or Thinkific.com or use online platforms like Udemy.com. Once you create an online course, it can work for you while you sleep!

BUILD AN APP

Apps can be a very lucrative passive income source. Practically everyone you can image has a smartphone so building an app can potentially reach far and wide! Apps pretty much make people's lives easier so if you can find an idea that can serve a need then you have struck gold. There is a lot of competition out there but If you can come up with something unique, you can definitely make a profit. As far as creating the app, you can either learn how to code or hire a designer but either way it shouldn't be too expensive or labor intensive.

BECOME AN INFLUENCER

The word influencer gets tossed around pretty often now in days but if you have highly engaged followers; whether it's on your website or social media platforms, brands will pay you to get your followers to buy or try out their products or services. This passive income technique works well if you align yourself with brands that you use or are passionate about. Depending on how large your reach is, a brand may pay you a flat fee or a percentage of the amount of sales you were able to convert.

You can find affiliate partners by going to the brands directly or keeping an eye out on ads that are being served up to you or your audience.

Rental Income

This option is common in some circles, a secret in others but nonetheless my favorite. Even when the economy is doing badly you can manage to make a good return with little to no risk. The key is buying the right property in the right neighborhood, renting to the right tenant, and having the right company manage it (If you don't want to manage it yourself).

The first step is to find out the residential vacancy rate of a given rental market. This is a good indicator as to how often people move out of this neighborhood and gives you a realistic view on whether it's a good investment or not.

The second step is to find a property in this neighborhood. This process is slightly different from finding a primary residence. The main things you need to be concerned with are the condition of the property and whether the neighborhood has a low vacancy rate. One thing to keep in mind is that the property does not have to be close by. You can find excellent deals in other areas.

That leads me to step three, which is find a good property management company. A property management company can alleviate many of the stresses that come with being a landlord and gives you the opportunity to buy property in another city, state, or region without having to worry about maintaining the property. Just sit back, relax and collect a check. Most property management companies' charge a flat fee or percentages so do some research before obtaining one. It is a good idea to find a company that has a lot of experience managing properties in the area you are buying from. They would be better equipped to know what type of tenant to look for.

I had a friend who was into rental properties and since he lived in New York City where real estate was expensive, he decided to take a drive to upstate New York where the rental market was thriving. He was able to purchase a three-family home for $40,000 put $8,000 down, took out a mortgage for the rest and is paying less than $400 a month in monthly mortgage payments. He hires a management company who manages the property, charging a 10% fee. They helped him find three tenants who are paying $600 a month each for rent and now sits back and collects a $1200 check each month after all expenses are paid.

Franchise a Business

A franchise is simply a company that allows investors to buy and operate a store using their name in return for a fee and increase in name recognition. Franchising is another great way to create passive income. In order to become successful as a franchisee you must have some business savvy. Make sure that you research the franchise you are wanting to get involved with to assure that you understand the business inside and out. Whether its owning some Wing Stop's like Rick Ross or Five Guys Burgers and Fries like Shaq; getting into the right franchise can help you build your wealth tremendously.

Become a Silent Partner in a Business

Not everyone is fit to be a boss or entrepreneur but everyone should own a piece of a business. Becoming a silent partner in a business allows you to make your money work for you. If you know of a successful business that needs money to expand, you can become a small angel investor and earn some equity in return. This isn't about lending the business money because you want to be in it for the long haul so positioning this as a partnership will allow you to get paid off of the success of the business forever. When you are a silent partner in a business, the business owner or management team handles all of the day to day operations while you sit back a get your cut.

NETWORK MARKETING

Network marketing or Multi level marketing is the process of providing a product or service and recruiting its users to sell it to their network of friends, family, and co-workers hence building a multi level market. You are compensated through residual income based on how many people you have working under your network and how well they can recruit additional persons.

With the introduction of the internet we started to see pyramid schemes develop. A pyramid scheme basically involves the exchange of money for enrolling people into a program that offers money incentives in exchange for bringing in more people; no product or service is ever exchanged. These schemes mostly result in the person at the top receiving all of the monetary benefit.

In 2003, the United States Federal Trade Commission (FTC) cracked down on these pyramid schemes but by doing so they served a damaging blow to legitimate MLM companies like Amway, ACN, Mary Kay, Tupperware, and Avon. Nonetheless, network marketing if done right can create passive income with little to no work. It may require a lot of leg work in the beginning but once you get started it will produce remarkable results.

The key to avoiding pyramid schemes is to only work with companies that actually provide a product or service. For more information please read Be a Recruiting Superstar: The Fast Track to Network Marketing Millions by Mary Christensen.

**Note: As you begin to receive this passive income, you may grow an urge to treat yourself to the finer things in life; that's perfectly fine but keep your financial goals in mind. Spending money on luxuries is not forbidden as long as it's done in moderation. This shouldn't hurt your plan and in fact may produce the drive and incentive you need to continue to build passive income. Spending money on things that make you feel good is a great way to put you in the right appreciative state of mind but make sure that you are equally spending money on other income producing assets.

CHAPTER
5:42

Please don't die over the neighborhood

"We hustle out of a sense of hopelessness. Sort of a desperation. Through that desperation, we become addicted."

- JAY Z

Jay-Z discusses this important aspect of ownership by talking about a conversation he had with an unnamed person where he told him, "Please don't die over the neighborhood, that your mama rentin' Take your drug money and buy the neighborhood, That's how you rinse it" While some may frown upon Jay giving money advice to a drug dealer, you must realize that as a retired drug dealer himself and someone who has won and lost in the street life, he is encouraging other drug dealers to do the same... Retire! And as a master wordsmith when he says "Rinse it" he is using a play on words meaning to launder drug money, cleaning up the neighborhood, and also leasing the apartments for profit ("rents it").

As a community, there is a perception that the black inner-city neighborhoods are known for drug dealing, gang-banging, and turf wars. But why die over a neighborhood that your mama renting? The question is a deep thought of why would someone put their lives on the line for something they don't own.

Property ownership can be broken down into three categories; physical property, intellectual property and real property. Physical property refers to any tangible items such as cars, jewelry, clothes, etc.; Intellectual property is anything that is created by the mind such as music, poetry, art, and so forth. Real property refers to Real Estate and land either personally or commercially owned. While most physical property usually goes down in value, intellectual property and real property appreciates more often than not.

Owning property is one of the most important things a person can do while on the road to building wealth and finding financial freedom. Using Jay as an example, owning property did a few things for him. First it gave him full creative control over what he was producing musically; second it allowed him to take full advantage and reap most of the benefits of his hard work. Lastly, it created a source of wealth via intellectual property and other business ventures that go beyond just music.

His road to riches had many ups and downs and can be viewed as a difficult journey but by taking full ownership of everything he was doing, he was able to dictate how successful he would be, without having to compromise anything. Most people work hard to get into certain positions, then turnover all of their hard work into someone else's hands. Without ownership, your work can go in vain, forcing you to start over and leaving you depressed or unmotivated.

While I strongly encourage the ownership of property in all matters, for our purposes in this chapter we will be talking about the ownership of real property also known as home ownership (We'll talk about other types of ownerships in later chapters).

Home ownership is vital in creating personal wealth and financial freedom for the same reasons creative ownership helped benefit Jay-Z. Before we continue you must be aware of a few things: Home ownership is a long-term commitment. Before considering home ownership, you must make sure that it makes sense for your particular situation. If you are just getting settled in a career, a new relationship or a new business venture, I would suggest that you really plan and strategize before you jump into home ownership.

As we all know, the beginning of the recession of 2008 started with the collapse of the U.S. housing market. A lot of first time home owners were so eager to be part of the American dream that they either rushed or were duped into bad mortgages. As a result, the foreclosure rate went up by 225% since 2006. According to RealtyTrac, a real estate organization that specializes in foreclosures and bank repossession a total of 3.1 million households submitted foreclosure filings during the recession with a total of over 800,000 actually foreclosing.

These alarming numbers have surely frightened many would be home owners but it shouldn't. Nothing can ever take the place of planning. If you have created the habit of paying yourself first, you are religiously following your budget and created a sound plan for the future, the odds are you will know when you are ready to purchase that home. When that time comes, plan and do research as well as consult a professional for advice.

Besides the wealth building benefits that owning a home can provide, it also increases self- confidence, creates a positive environment, improves neighborhoods, and provides stability. In a study done by the Consumer Federation of America (CFA), it was concluded that over half of the personal wealth that is held by lower income households comes by way of home ownership and the equity that is accumulated in the home. Once a home is purchased and the mortgage is eventually paid in full, the value of the home becomes a source of wealth because of its ability to be sold for cash. For example, in 1970 a family could have purchased a brownstone in Harlem for only $26,000. Today that same brownstone is probably worth upwards of $2 million making that an increase of more than 7,600% and a form of generational wealth.

In fact, I was recently featured in Black Enterprise magazine discussing the importance of home ownership and wealth. In the feature, I discuss how the majority of wealth is accumulated through home appreciation, yet, blacks are lagging significantly behind. According to a report released by the U.S. census Bureau titled 2013 Wealth and Asset Ownership Detailed Tables, the median net worth of African-American households was $9,211 and $12,460 for Hispanic households; – which are significant gaps from the median net worth of $132,483 for white households. What is interesting about this report is that if you excluded equity from home ownership, African-American households would have a median net worth of only $2,725, $5,825 for Hispanic households and $51,100 for white households; proving how much home ownership is vital to creating family wealth.

Even if a home is still being paid off, the money that is paid to the mortgage minus the interest, goes back to the homeowner as equity. There are also many tax benefits and savings that are provided to home owners, giving them two opportunities to build wealth. The tax benefits include savings from mortgage interest, property tax, and other payments associated with financing your home by way of tax deductions. Those who are renters allow the tax savings of home ownership to go to their landlord. The average tax savings for a homeowner is about 12% which is equivalent to $120 for every $1,000 paid towards your home. If the home is never sold, it can be passed down from generation to generation giving the beneficiary access to more money to use to build wealth.

And how does this translate into breaking the cycle of poverty? Well according to a study done by Boehm and Schlottmann as well as the University of Tennessee, it states that children of homeowners are 59% more likely to become homeowners. Their children are also 25% more likely to graduate from high school and 116% more likely to graduate from college. A study done by www.Fightcrime.org shows that a 10% increase in graduation rates would result in fewer murders and fewer aggravated assaults each year.

Homeownership has also been shown to improve neighborhoods. It is a fact that in recent years home ownership in disadvantaged, low income neighborhoods have been increasing, while crime in those same areas have been decreasing. Groups who advocate for community reinvestment as well as many law enforcement agencies have argued for years that access to banks, home ownership and small businesses are very important to the stability of a neighborhood.

In a 2000 census report, researchers analyzed the small business and home lending trends and compared them to the national crime report and found that as one increased the other decreased. These results prove that there is a direct correlation between home ownership and low crime.

The point is simply that home ownership teaches responsibility. When something is yours and you know that you worked hard for it, you tend to treat it better and develop a stronger sense of appreciation for it and its surroundings. You now have a stake in the community which makes people more involved in civic affairs, the school system and of course crime reduction. The absence of a negative environment has a trickle-down effect on your overall well-being, your stress level and ultimately your finances. Home ownership is more than just owning a piece of property, psychologically it can change the way people value themselves and their community. Those two paradigm shifts can create wealth for generations and break the cycle of poverty.

Depending on where you are in your life right now, homeownership may not be for you at this moment, but in planning for your financial future this must be a part of that plan. We all must strive for home ownership at some point in our lives but I can't stress enough how much you must really be ready before you jump in. There are many people who don't support the notion of homeownership at all, and if you were to do an internet search on the pros and cons you would have more people against it than for it. This is because most people have believed many of the myths and lies told about homeownership and have used this as a way to force us into complacency and continue the cycle of not generating wealth.

The following are myths often stated about homeownership:

Myth #1: Owning a home costs too much and comes with too many responsibilities

It's believed that owning a home costs too much money and the work it takes to maintain it would be too time-consuming. In some cases, owning a home will cost you more than renting but you'll be surprised at how many times it's actually quite the opposite.

As we speak, in New York City there is someone paying rent of $1,600 a month for a two-bedroom apartment. A few blocks away there is a two-bedroom condo for sale in the same neighborhood for $200,000 with $418 maintenance charge each month. If you were to obtain a mortgage at 4% interest putting only 5% down ($10,000); your monthly mortgage payment including maintenance, taxes and insurance would equal to $1,481. That is a savings of $119 a month. In this scenario, a renter has spent $19,200 a year in an apartment and they will never see a dime of that money back; opposed to the $17,772 invested on home ownership that will more than likely be available in the home as equity which can be borrowed against in the future.

As far as maintaining the property, if you live in a co-op or condo there is a maintenance fee that is assessed each month that covers most damages. With homes, the maintenance required isn't as much as people make it seem. Yes, if something breaks you are responsible for it but that is a small price to pay for all the benefit you get from owning.

Myth #2: You need great credit to become a homeowner.

It is a common misconception that you must have impeccable credit in order to qualify for a mortgage. In fact, it is much more difficult to obtain a personal loan or car loan than it is to get a mortgage. As we stated before a car depreciates as soon as you drive it off the lot; for that reason, a bank wants to be certain that the loan can be repaid. With a mortgage, the home is the collateral, which usually appreciates with time so a bank is more willing to approve those types of loans knowing that if you default they can always take the home back, sell it, and still make their money.

Keep in mind that even though you are able to afford a home now with less-than-perfect credit, make sure that you are working towards repairing your credit and that those costs are included in your budget. I also strongly advise you to speak with a housing counsellor to help you avoid getting a mortgage you can't afford. Sometimes when you have less-than-perfect credit you feel vulnerable and feel that you have to go with the first bank that grants you approval. Stop! Do your research first and find out what each bank's guidelines are before making a commitment. Again, you will be surprised at how great of a deal you can get with less-than perfect credit.

Myth #3: You need a lot of money for the down payment.

A 20% down payment is usually the standard amount needed to purchase a home but not always the requirement. What some people don't know is that there are many types of mortgage products and programs that allow you to put a low down payment or even none at all. With some of those programs it is important that you understand that your interest rate may be higher but in most cases, it's still affordable.

The Home Buying Process
Step 1: Determine if you are ready

The reason why we saw so many foreclosures in the past was because most families were anxious to live the American dream but negated to properly plan or misunderstood the commitment that was needed to become a homeowner. Before you become a homeowner, there is important planning that has to be done to determine if you are ready. The first step is to have an idea of the type of home you are looking to purchase (i.e. Co-op, condo, 1 family home, 2 family home, etc.) which is usually based on a combination of your current and future lifestyle. Do what makes sense for you now but be sure to plan for your future as well. If you anticipate any major life events such as marriage, the birth of a child, relocation, career change and so forth, it would be advisable to wait until that settles down before you pursue home ownership.

After you decide on the type of home you want, you then need to calculate your income, savings, monthly expenses, and debt. If you're following your budget as instructed earlier these things should be readily available. This will determine if you need a mortgage to finance the home and if so how much in monthly mortgage payments you can afford without drastically affecting your budget. Keep in mind that if you do need a mortgage you will need money for down payment, closing cost, as well as an emergency fund. With that in mind, the purchase of a home should in no way deplete all of your savings. After doing the calculations, if it does than you are not ready! You should continue to save your money.

Most mortgage companies require a 20% down payment of the purchase price of the home but there are programs that may allow you to make a smaller down payment. In those cases, you may be asked to pay what's called Private Mortgage Insurance (PMI) which is insurance that protects the lender from defaults. Sometimes you can also have the closing costs rolled into the mortgage, which is a good option if available so that you can have more of your money reserved for emergencies and continue your wealth building.

Step 2: Check your qualifications

Once you've calculated all the information in step 1 it is now time for us to make sure you qualify for a loan. The factors that most lending institutions use to determine eligibility is credit, debt-to-income ratio, loan-to-value, and savings.

Credit: Each lender has a minimum credit score that an applicant must have in order to obtain a mortgage so check with your lender to determine what is an acceptable score.

Debt-to-Income ratio: Your debt-to-income ratio or DTI is what banks use to determine how big of a loan you can handle as it relates to your debt obligations.

Because your monthly housing payments will include Principal, Interest, Taxes and Insurance payments (PITI) and other household expenses, your DTI must establish that you can handle the additional expense. Your debt-to-income ratio score has a big impact on the lender's decision to provide the loan or not. There isn't a standard ratio; each lender or loan program has their own rules regarding the percentage of income that can be applied toward your monthly house payment. At one point, most banks required a DTI of 45% or less but they now look for lower. Again, each institution has its own guidelines so do your research.

Loan-to-Value: Loan-to-value is simply the percentage of the loan as it relates to the value of the home. For example, if you are buying a home that is valued at $100,000 and you put $20,000 as a down payment you would need a mortgage of $80,000. Your loan-to-value would be 80% because of the $80,000 loan divided by the $100,000 value. This ratio is important because most lenders will not lend more than the home is worth. Some do, but in those cases, it's only up to 6% to cover closing cost. If the value of the home again is $100,000 and you wanted a loan of $140,000. No bank would ever approve this mortgage because it would equate to a 140% LTV and the maximum a bank would do is 106% (a 106% loan would mean that the buyer has put zero money down and is even including their closing cost in the loan. At one point this was possible but lenders are rarely giving out these types of mortgages any longer because of the amount of foreclosures we've seen as of late). Please don't confuse value with sale price as some do. If the home was worth $100,000 but a seller was selling it for $70,000 it is possible to take out a mortgage for $80,000 because the LTV would be 80% giving you $10,000 cash back at closing.

Savings: Lenders need to see what money you have saved in order to determine loan eligibility as well. Your savings can be used to offset your DTI if it's too high. Having significant savings shows the bank that you have something to rely on in the event that you lose your source of income.

Step 3: Figure out what your Cash Requirements are

It's important to know how much of your savings is going to go to upfront costs that are associated with buying a home; those costs include closing cost, and down payments. You must also make sure that you will have money left over to cover all housing expenses as well as non-housing expenses. Most banks want potential homeowners to have at least three months of living expenses available after closing on the loan but I suggest at least six to eight months.

Up-front cash requirements include:

Closing Costs - closing cost consist of any fees that have to be paid by the buyer to conclude the sale. This includes lawyer fees, bank fees, property tax, insurance, and escrow. Your closing costs will differ depending on where you decide to purchase your home and what type of loan program you get. It's possible to negotiate lower closing cost with the seller and lender or even finance some portion of the closing costs as part of the loan. The option that you pick is determined by what works best for you and your financial situation. Consult with a mortgage loan officer to determine which option is the best.

Down Payment - As stated previously your down payment is a percentage of the sale price that is paid up-front and can also differ based on lender, location, and loan program. In most cases, the more you put down the more you can negotiate a lower interest rate. Again, you shouldn't deplete all of your savings to become a homeowner but if you find yourself falling short there are many places you can receive assistance. Monetary gifts from family members are one option as well as borrowing from friends or relatives. I have a pet peeve about borrowing money from friends and family but it is an option nonetheless. Some people choose to borrow from their retirement funds such as their 401k. Sometimes this is the best option because the money you pay back towards the loan goes back to your 401k. Either way, no matter where you decide to borrow the money from, remember to include this new expense into your budget. One last option would be Down Payment Assistance Programs. These programs are usually set up by not-for-profit, for profit and government agencies. The Federal Housing Administration (FHA) and the Department of Veterans Affairs (VA) are two government agencies that offer down payment assistance. You can also contact your local Department of Housing and Urban Development (HUD) to find out what programs they have.

Overall finding out your cash requirement is an important part of planning to become a homeowner and affords you the benefit of knowing all of your cash needs upfront rather than being surprised later.

Step 4: See what Loan Programs you qualify for

FHA LOAN: FHA loans are mortgage programs that are available to low and moderate-income families who are credit worthy but don't qualify for a regular mortgage. There are significant benefits such as being allowed to make a 3.5% down payment to finance closing costs and a set limit on the amount banks can charge for some closing cost fees. FHA loans allow credit scores between 500 and 579 but those who fall under those scores have to put at least 10% down. The maximum mortgage amount allowed can differ significantly depending on where you buy.

VA LOANS: Eligible veterans can purchase a home with a VA loan program called "The VA guaranty loan". This program makes it easier for veterans to obtain mortgages because it provides protection to the banks in the event the veterans can't pay their loan.

VA loans are extremely beneficial for those veterans who don't have a lot of money available to purchase a home. The benefits of the VA loan allow the ability to purchase with no down payment, provides better interest rates, and also gives the option of financing closing cost.

A Veteran is described as anyone who has served on active duty and has a discharge other than dishonorable. There are guidelines on the amount of time you have to serve to be eligible but please visit your local VA office for more information.

Step 5: See How Much Home You Can Afford

Knowing how much home you can afford is a very important part of the home buying process. It affects your budget and can affect your piece of mind. There are many mortgage calculators that can be used in order to know what you can afford but before you use one, you must do some preliminary calculations. The standard percentage of your income that goes to housing expenses should be 28%. In calculating, make sure that your monthly payments don't go beyond that.

Remember that your mortgage payments include taxes, insurance, and maintenance or dues if applicable so take that into consideration as well. Visit www.Bankrate.com for a good version of a mortgage calculator.

Step 6: Understand Mortgage Options

Understanding your mortgage options is a very important part of the home buying process. The repercussions of not knowing are severe and can make the difference between the process being a dream or a nightmare. Most of the debacle of the mortgage industry was a result of many home buyers getting into loans that they didn't understand. They entered into loan agreements that initially had low monthly payments but within a couple of years it ballooned into payments that were three-times the original amount. With this unexpected and unmanageable increase, many were forced to abandon their dreams and face the embarrassing and life shattering process of foreclosure. Many of these families spent years saving for this dream and in a blink of an eye it was all gone. The following is a brief description and explanation of different types of mortgages.

Fixed-Rate Mortgage: A Fixed-Rate Mortgage is an easy and straightforward loan and is the most common of them all. It is a mortgage that has the same interest rate for the life of the loan hence the title fixed-rate. Your payment remains the same and doesn't go up or down no matter what is happening in the economy. If you luck out and get one of these loans while interest rates are low, you'll continue to pay that rate even if rates increase significantly. On the other hand, if you take one of these loans while rates are high and later on rates decrease you're locked in at the higher rate. In this situation, the only way out of that type of loan is to refinance which may incur additional fees. Fixed-rate mortgages are the most secure kind of loan a buyer can get because you'll always know what you are paying with no unexpected surprises. The risk to the bank is higher, because it loses the opportunity to take advantage of market fluctuations. Because of this, fixed-rate mortgage rates are usually higher than the other type of mortgages.

Adjustable Rate Mortgage: An Adjustable Rate Mortgage or ARM as it is usually referred to, is exactly what the name implies. It is a mortgage that does not have a fixed-rate and adjusts based on how interest rates fluctuate. An ARM provides the buyer with a lower initial monthly payment than that of a fixed rate loan. The rate is usually about 2 percentage points lower. This lower payment gives the buyer the ability to qualify for a higher loan amount. It also gives the buyer the opportunity to receive even lower interest payments if the interest rate drops. On the flip side, your payments can go up if interest rates rise, but there are caps that limit the interest from rising out of control. One thing that you must be aware of is that the initial lower interest rate and monthly payments are only temporary and will more than likely go up. If you don't anticipate this increase you can be setting yourself up for a disaster. Typically, ARM's are a great option for those who don't intend on keeping the home for a long period of time. If you are buying real estate to flip then an ARM is the best way to go. People who receive large bonuses or are anticipating receiving a large sum of money and intend to pay the home off soon would also be a good fit. Regardless of your situation be sure to consult with a mortgage professional prior to making a decision.

Mortgage Terms: The two most common mortgage terms are 30-year and 15-year. Some banks have introduced 20-year and 40-year terms but those are not the norm. Because you are stretching your loan out over a longer period of time, a 30-year loan typically has a lower monthly payment than a 15-year. If you are able to handle the payments of a 15-year mortgage term, which is significantly higher, you will wind up saving a lot of money because you are cutting your interest payments in half. When it comes to terms, there is no such thing as a right or wrong option, it again depends on what you can afford.

Rates and Points: The interest rate that you receive for your loan is mostly dependent on the economy and whether rates are high or low. These factors are beyond your control so it's mostly luck and timing that assist in getting a great rate. The only control you have as it relates to your rate is by way of points. A point is equal to 1% of your loan and usually reduces your rate by an eighth of a percentage point. An example of how a discount point would work would be if you were trying to get a loan for $100,000. Each "point" would cost you 1% of $100,000 or $1,000 which at the same time would reduce your rate by .125%. With this point structure the bank could offer you a 4.0% loan with zero points, a 3.875% loan with one point, or a 3.75% loan with 2 points. The fees for the points are paid at closing but sometimes the bank may let you put the fee into your loan. Be careful with banks that try to make their rates seem lower by using points. Make sure when you are comparing rates you take the points into consideration.

There are other types of loans available but in order to fully understand your options its best to speak with a mortgage consultant. Do not get into a loan that you do not understand. Buying a home is not about trust. It's about understanding your options, then making an informed decision. This is your future and your financial freedom at stake! If you don't understand something, ask questions. If you still don't understand, ask more questions!

Step 7: Research neighborhoods and schools

Owning a home shouldn't just be about owning a piece of property, it's about owning an experience. It's about creating a better environment for yourself and your family. Because homeownership is such a long-term commitment you have to make sure that you research the neighborhood and school district before you decide to purchase. School ratings, crime rates and appreciation rates are the main things you should look for. School ratings provide a sense of what the parenting and care is like in the neighborhood. Schools with the highest ratings are usually the ones where the parents are more involved. Parental involvement often means community involvement which gives you an indication that the neighborhood will be safe.

Crime rates are important for obvious reasons; no one wants to live in a negative environment. The trickle-down effect on crime to your finances and quality of living are so important that you must not put yourself in that situation. Appreciation rates give you an indication of how popular your new neighborhood is. Those neighborhoods with high appreciation rates are often the safest and tell a story about how easy it would be to get a return on your investment in the event that you want to sell. There are other factors to consider as well, such as travel time to work, neighborhood demographic and transportation need.

Home ownership is supposed to be about being comfortable and enjoying your surroundings. Some people neglect these other factors as if they aren't important but if you are not comfortable with your neighborhoods demographic, if the travel time to work is too much or if you don't consider your transportation needs, you will be stuck in an unnecessary stressful situation. Finding a home is like finding a soul mate. Make sure you go on a couple of dates and get to know the neighborhood before you marry it. You should do some preliminary research about the neighborhood first. Sites like www.NeighborhoodScout.com can be a great source of initial research but nothing takes the place of real life experience. Be sure to visit the neighborhood, and schools in person. Give yourself a real sense of how it would feel living in that neighborhood.

Step 8: Find A Good Real Estate Agent:

Having a good real estate agent during the home buying process is like having a good lawyer while going to court or having a good doctor if you're sick. A real estate agent is the person that helps find you a property and ensures that you get a good deal. This person gets paid to advocate for buyers and sellers and because you will probably only go through the home buying process once or twice you need someone who has the experience of negotiating with other agents, buyers and sellers. Just as in any profession there are going to be people out there who abuse their power and try to take advantage of people. It's for this exact reason that you must also do research when looking for a real estate agent.

The best and most effective way to find one is by word of mouth. If you have friends, family or co-workers who have gone through the home buying process they will be glad to refer you their agent if he or she did a good job. By using someone who has a track record of success you increase your chances of being satisfied. A referral is a reflection of the referrer's character and judgment so no one would refer someone that didn't really do a good job. Make sure you meet with the agent before you make a commitment to work with them. You will be spending a lot of time with this person so make sure that your personalities are a good fit. Interview this person, ask them about how they find properties and make sure their presentation skills are up to par. Another great way to make sure this agent is a right fit is to watch them in action. Attend an open house for a client that the agent already has, watch how they interact with their current clients and see how knowledgeable they are about the property. Did they do their homework? Or are they just winging it? If you can't find a real estate agent through word of mouth you can always visit your local real estate office and ask for a referral. Make sure you go through the same interview process when being referred someone from the real estate office. Once you find that perfect match, it's time to let them work!

Step 9: Make an offer:

After carefully researching different neighborhoods and finding a home that suits your wants and needs, the next step would be to make an offer. This step is going to require the experience, expertise, and negotiation skills of your agent. Once you're ready to make an offer this will clearly state to the seller what you're willing to pay and what are the conditions. Some homes are bought as is, some require repairs to be done; this all will be specified in the offer.

In particular a written offer usually includes the complete legal description of the home, the amount of money that will be given upfront also known as earnest money, details on how the home will be financed, the proposed move-in date, the closing date, and of course the price you are offering. When coming up with a reasonable price, you and your agent must understand what homes sell for in that area, what condition is the home in, how long the seller has been trying to sell, what are the financing terms, and the seller's situation. The seller's situation and the length of time the home has been on the market are very important bargaining tools, so don't take those lightly.

At this point you've already figured out how much you can afford so make sure your agent understands your limit as well. I caution anyone who wants to handle this portion of the process themselves. This is a very important part and can either cost you or save you thousands of dollars, so don't rush and let the expert handle the business.

There are going to be situations where you are looking to purchase a home in a hot real estate market where the houses are selling fast. In those cases, you want to make your offer as soon as possible. This is where your agents' expertise will come in handy. They'll be able to provide you with an accurate offer in a timely manner. Make sure your agent does his/her research. You must compare the house for sale against recent sales in the area; your agent should have this information ready. If the seller wants more than what similar homes in the area recently sold for, you should offer lower than what they're asking, using the recent sales as your rational.

Once your offer is made, be prepared with a plan B just in case your offer is turned down or if the seller has multiple buyers. You have to anticipate all of these situations and be ready with a plan if it happens. When in doubt listen to your agent. They don't get paid unless the home is sold so it is in their best interest to make sure that your offer gets accepted.

Step 10: Close the Deal:

Now that the seller has accepted your offer, it is now time to get ready to close the deal. Before you do this, you must get the home appraised and inspected. A home appraisal is set by the bank to assure that the home is worth at least what you are paying for it. In most cases, it is worth more but it cannot be worth less. The inspection is also needed by the bank to determine the worth of the home but this is an important report for you as well.

You never want to buy someone else's problems unless you are told upfront and are being compensated for it. For example, if you are purchasing a home and the inspector says that the boiler is only going to last another year, you may want to renegotiate the sale price to reflect the cost that you are going to have to shell out to get the boiler replaced. Once the keys are turned over to you, everything in the house becomes your responsibility. The inspection is a vital step to assure that you are getting what you pay for. Your Real Estate Agent will be equipped to refer you to a good inspector. Because they are in the business of selling homes they meet many inspectors and build great relationships. These relationships will assure that you will get the best inspector with the most experience.

Closing: Closing simply means that the buyer and the seller will sign the documents needed to legally transfer the ownership of the property from one person to the next. During a closing, the parties that are usually involved are the buyer, the buyer's attorney, the buyer's agent, the seller, the seller's attorney, the seller's agent, the title company and the closing attorney. The role of the closing attorney is to represent the bank and protect its interest in the loan so in no way can they give you any legal advice.

Before you close you need to get homeowners insurance and have proof and agree to keep the home insured after the closing. The insurance has to show the bank as the loss payee which means that if anything were to happen to the home the bank would be protected against any loss. If the terms of your offer have changed for whatever reasons, make sure that all parties involved are aware including the bank. This may have an effect on the loan amount or fees, so there has to be enough time given to make the adjustments. If you are having issues in regards to the contract terms, price negotiations and repairs that have to be done make sure this is also taken care of before the closing. Your loan officer at the bank will also advise you on the estimated amount of money needed at closing. Please keep in mind that this is just an estimate so be prepared to pay more or less.

During the closing, you must be present with photo identification and a cashier's check for any money that has to be paid. Consult with your bank to find out who you should make it payable to. If the check is too much, you will be given a refund and if it is not enough you can write a personal check for the difference, so make sure you bring your checkbook. Your bank may also need you to bring additional documents but they will notify ahead of time. Everyone will also review the HUD-1 Settlement Statement which is the report that details all the costs associated with the closing. Any adjustments to the HUD-1 that are needed will be made at closing. You should and have the right to read all of your closing documents before you sign them but if you decide not to, the closing attorney will give you concise explanations of every document.

Once the closing is done the closing attorney is responsible for recording the sale with the county, sending you a completed loan package, and disbursing all monies to the respected party as per the HUD-1 Settlement Statement.

Congratulations!! You are now a home owner!! Enjoy your new home, your new life and your new piece of mind! You are well on your way to financial freedom!

Take Real Chances Over Advances

"'Til you own your own, you can't be free"

- JAY Z

I once read a Facebook post that pretty much sums up what Jay is saying throughout the entire album; It stated, "While we (blacks) were being told to go to college, get a corporate job, dress like, walk like, talk like... others, the Vietnamese were opening nails salons. The Koreans opened beauty supply stores. The Chinese opened restaurants. The Arabs opened gas stations. The Jewish opened record labels and made money strictly off of black folks and they dressed like, walked like, and talked like themselves." When Jay asked, "Y'all out here still takin' advances, huh?" He was simply pointing out that in this day and age with all of the access and resource readily available to everyone, we must recognize our power and stop allowing ourselves to be pimped.

Let me step back for a second... An "advance" is money that is borrowed from a record label that artists must pay back. Advances are usually given to an artist prior to them putting out any music with the record label, so advances are usually a good way to fund an artist before they start making money. This made sense because the record label wants the artist to focus on music, so they pay them some of what they expect the artist to make, prior to them making it, hence why it's called an advance. The problem with advances is that the concept is old and unnecessary and it now controls you and makes you beholden to the label because you owe them money.

As Jay said in I got the keys, "Until you own your own, you can't be free." Another reason why advances aren't really a good idea is because with so many ways for artist to get paid independently, artist should focus more on building their fan base to make money doing what they love so that if signing with a label is an option that they want to pursue later, the artist would have more leverage to negotiate and get what they are really worth. Similar to the story Master P gave as to why he turned down a $1 million-dollar deal from Jimmy Lovine and Interscope when he only had $500 to his name; P states, "I knew if Interscope were willing to pay me $1 million, I could make $40 million if I figured out how to own my talent."

Basically, Jay was warning new artists to stay away from accepting advances. Simply put, he wants them to realize that they don't need to sign record deals anymore because of the many ways an artist can make money on their own. Jay-Z and his team uses their own money to fund their entrepreneurial ventures. This has been their model from day one, so when he says, "Me and my n@%$as takin' real chances, uh," he is not exaggerating. In fact, those real chances that he and his n@%$as been taking, has allowed him to amass a net worth of $810 million as of May 2017, and his team isn't starving either.

Using Lauryn Hill as a prime example of why most record labels are shady. Jay poses the question "After what they done to our Lauryn Hill?" Did you know that in 1998, Lauryn was sued by her own label for "using their songs and production skills and failing to credit them properly." She also had many other problems with her label throughout her career where they were trying to restrict her artistic freedom, hence why she only had one classic album.

It should not take neither Jay nor I need to convince you that record labels are notoriously known for cheating their artists out of millions, all you have to do is watch a music biopic and you'll get the point. But just for reference and to recognize,

Jay-Z's word wizardry, look up Norman Lear, so you will understand why he said "F@#k a piece of the pie, I want the whole cake." Then research Jimmy Iovine, Jay-Z, and Apple to understand why he shows Jimmy respect but tells him in the same line that this is a whole new regime. Lastly, lookup Lucian Grainge and Doug Morris to put context to the line "Lucian is cool. But Lucian don't write, Doug ain't this tight." Simply put, too many people are profiting off of the talent of others because the talent doesn't recognize it's worth.

This brings me back to why I said earlier that "we must recognize our power and stop allowing ourselves to be pimped." Jay-Z is a music artist at heart so of course he will talk specifically to artist, but this is happening beyond just music; it happens in sports, in film, in business, and in any other genre you can think of. To pimp a butterfly, was Kendrick Lamar's second album and while there are many interpretations of what he meant by that title, think about it for a second: How can you pimp a butterfly? Why would a butterfly allow itself to be pimped? The butterfly is beautiful on its own, it can fly on its own, and it can do great things on its own! Why does a butterfly need a pimp? It doesn't, but the fact remains that once you get into a butterfly's head, you can convince him/her that it needs assistance to be great. That is what happens to many of us. We allow others to convince us that we need them in order to realize our greatness when we were born with our greatness already intact. It's time to stop being pimped and take a chance on you!

The only way for you to truly get what you deserve out of life is to not be afraid to put it all on the line for yourself. Understand your gift and use that to create financial freedom. Don't sell the gift for pennies when it's worth way more. When Jay-Z first came on the scene, he didn't sign to a label; instead he and his team created partnerships with labels and other businesses. This is the difference between being a worker or a boss. A worker is at the mercy of what the boss says and has to follow orders, a boss still has people to report to, but in a different capacity. The boss has the idea and aligns that idea with people who can help turn that idea into a lucrative business.

Don't get me mistaken, there is nothing wrong with being a worker; that just can't be your long-term strategy. Your higher power has placed a gift inside of you that you must materialize at some point or you are just wasting your life. Whether it's music, film, technology, books, clothes, or any other gift you have, make sure that you take the appropriate steps to become the master of your fate.

According to the Small Business Administration, there are more than 28 million small businesses in the United States, making up an astounding 99.7 percent of all U.S. businesses, so when you think of it, the lifeblood of our country's economy is based on the ideas and execution of people like you and I. Let's be real though, entrepreneurship isn't for everybody. In fact, only about two-thirds of businesses with employees survive at least two years, and about half survive five years.

The truth of the matter is that some people who attempt being their own boss may wind up broke, depressed and ready to quit at times; that's why it is important that when you take the leap, you do so in the right way. For some, the right way may be to quit your job and become an entrepreneur full-time and for others it may mean to start your business on the side as you continue to work.

No matter what direction your chose the following are 10 steps you need to take to properly start your business:

Step 1: Research Your Business Idea

Everyone has a million-dollar idea in their head but sometimes when you put it on paper it may not be all that you thought it might be. This doesn't mean to abandon the thought but it does mean that you should flesh out your idea to make sure that you are setting yourself up for success. Does your idea solve a problem, fulfill a need or offer something the market wants? If you answered yes to one or all of these questions then keep going. If not, then it may be time to test your idea to see if it makes sense to continue in its present form or do you need to revamp the idea.

Start by asking yourself a few questions: Is there a need for my product or service? If yes, then who needs it? Am I the first person to the market with this product or service or are there other companies offering a similar item? What is the competition like? How will my business fit into the market? What is my unique factor? The research you do to come up with these answers will be vital. You can also run focus groups or tease your product or service to see who is interested.

Step 2: Create Your Master Plan

Once you have confirmed the viability of your idea, it's time to create a business plan to map out how you will make your idea a reality. A business plan is a blueprint that will guide your business from the beginning to end, and it is necessary for all new businesses. As the saying goes, if you fail to plan then you plan to fail, so make sure you don't skip this step. There are different types of business plans for different types of businesses, so make sure you research and find the business plan template that fits your business.

If you are planning to raise money from an investor or borrow from a financial institution, a traditional business plan is a must. This type of business plan is usually long (pause) and thorough and has a common set of sections that investors and banks look for when they are validating your idea.

If you are not pitching to investors or banks then a simple one-page business plan can give you the clarity you need to achieve the goals that you set out for your business. Please visit www.IamAshCash.com/forms for access to sample business plan templates.

Step 3: Get Your Money Right

The amount of money needed to start a business from scratch will depend on the type of business you intend to begin. In most cases you will need some initial seed money to cover ongoing expenses before you turn a profit. It is important that you understand what your money needs are, before you start to run your business.

Begin by putting together a spreadsheet that estimates all of the one-time startup costs for your business; This may include licenses and permits, equipment, legal fees, insurance, branding, market research, inventory, trademarking, grand opening events, property leases, etc. If you are simply opening an online business you must still estimate your cost as well. You should also estimate how much you will need to run your business for at least 12 months. This should include rent, utilities, marketing and advertising, production, supplies, travel expenses, employee salaries, your own salary, etc. When you add all of those numbers up this is what you will need as your initial investment.

Now that you know how much money you need to get your business off of the ground, you should begin to bootstrap (which means using your money, and that of your friends and family if needed.) If you aren't able to raise enough money from your efforts then you have other options like small business loans, small business grants, angel investors, and crowdfunding. Visit www.sba.gov/funding-programs for access to funding opportunities.

Step 4: Pick a Business Structure

Your business structure is very important. This is what will determine what your legal responsibilities are as a business and/or as an individual (If you choose). Your business structure will also determine how you file your taxes. You can choose between sole proprietorship, partnership, limited liability company (LLC) or a corporation.

If you register as a sole proprietor you are indicating that you are taking full responsibility for the business personally, as there is no separation. Simply put a sole proprietorship is owned and run by one natural person. There is also no legal distinction between the owner and the business entity.

A partnership is an association of two or more people or entities that conduct a business for profit as co-owners.

A limited liability company (LLC) is exactly what the name implies; it is a company that limits your liability. Technically, a limited liability company (LLC) is a corporate structure where the members of the company cannot be held personally responsible or in legal terms "liable" for the company's debts or liabilities. Many people choose this structure because it is a hybrid entity that combines the characteristics of a corporation and a partnership or sole proprietorship

A corporation is a company or group of people authorized to act as a single entity. It is legally a person and is recognized as such in law. Corporations are owned by their stockholders (shareholders) who share in the profits and losses of the company through the firm's operations. Corporations have three distinct characteristics (1) Legal existence: a firm can (like a person) buy, sell, own, enter into a contract, and sue other persons and firms, and be sued by them. It can do good and be rewarded, and can commit offence and be punished. (2) Limited liability: a firm and its owners are limited in their liability to the creditors and other obligors only up to the resources of the firm, unless the owners give personal-guaranties. (3) Continuity of existence: a firm can live beyond the life spans and capacity of its owners, because its ownership can be transferred through a sale or gift of shares.

Once you choose your initial business structure, it is very well possible to change your structure as your business grows but make sure you consult with an attorney or CPA to make sure you are choosing the right structure for your business.

Step 5: Register Your Business Name

Your name is your name! (Marlo voice). Your business name will play a role in almost every aspect of your business including marketing and promotions, so make sure the name you choose can stand the test of time. After you picked a name, check to see if it's currently in use or trademarked. If the name is good to go, then, you will need to register it.

A sole proprietor must register their business name with either their state or county clerk. Corporations, LLCs, or limited partnerships typically register their business name when the formation paperwork is filed and you pay your State filing fee. Formation Documents are state-specific forms that officially create your entity. These documents are often referred to as your Articles of Organization, Certificate of Organization, or Certificate of Formation.

Make sure you also register your domain name once you have selected your business name.

Step 6: Get Permission to Operate (If Applicable)

Some types of businesses require licenses and/or permits to operate depending on where you are located. Make sure you research to see if this applies to you.

Step 7: Keep track of your finances

Men Lie, women Lie, numbers don't! The rise or fall of your business will begin and end with your numbers and the system you have in place to monitor those numbers. Managing your budget, setting your rates and prices, and filing your taxes are just a few examples of why your bookkeeping or accounting system is vital to the success of your business. From the outset, you should decide whether you will set up your accounting system yourself or if you will hire an accountant. No matter what you decide, your system is important and NEEDS to be put in place.

Step 8: Setup Your Physical Location

Just like how numbers don't lie, vibes don't lie either. Where your business is located and where it operates is super important so make sure you are keeping this in mind when starting your business. Whether its setting up a home office, working out of a starbucks, a coworking space, private office, or a retail location, know what location option works best for your pockets but also for your business vibe. How you feel when you are running your business will help with its success.

Step 9: Build Your Squad

Who are the people who will be helping you reach the promised land? Will you hire a management team or will you bring in business partners? Will you hire employees or will you outsource work to independent contractors? Do you have a business mentor or will you hire a coach? Your team matters! Your support system matters!

If you are hiring a management team or bringing in business partners, make sure you pick people whose vision and passion align with yours. This is your baby so "you can't just be having anybody around your children" (excuse the grammar).

Whether you are hiring employees or outsourcing work to independent contractors, make sure you take time to outline the positions you need to fill, and the job responsibilities that are part of each position. Also make sure you work with an attorney to get your independent contractor agreement in place if that's the direction you decide to go.

Lastly, make sure you create your own support team. This team can be comprised of a business mentor, small business coach, or even your family and friends to serve as your go to for advice, motivation and reassurance when the going gets tough.

Step 10: Spread the Word

What good is a diamond nobody can see? (Joe voice). Now that you have put in all of this work building a solid business foundation, it is time to spread the word and start attracting clients and customers. Start by creating a marketing plan to guide you on how to promote your business most effectively. Social media is your friend too, so make sure Twitter, Instagram, and Facebook are part of your outreach plans. visit www.IamAshCash.com/forms to download a marketing plan template.

Please keep in mind that no one owes you anything. So, anyone who supports your business is to be appreciated. The following are things you should keep in mind when dealing with customers in your business:

- Your customer is the most important person in your business. Without the customer, you have no business

- You are dependent on your customer not the other way around.

- A paying customer is never an interruption.

- Your customer is doing you a favor when they point out anything you can do better with your business. You should not take offense to their critique.

- Your customer is part of your business, not an outsider and should be treated as such.

One last word... Success doesn't happen overnight! Use these steps to set you on the right track but understand that your commitment and dedication to your business will determine your success. Stay busy, stay working, and treat your first like your last and your last like your first!

This Spiritual Stuff Really Works

"I believe everyone in the world is born with genius-level talent. Apply yourself to whatever you're genius at, and you can do anything in the world."

- JAY Z

As a guy who was raised by a single mom in the St. Nicholas Housing projects in Harlem, NY; I am intrigued and inspired by this enlightened multi-millionaire business mogul named Shawn Carter who is from the Marcy Housing projects in Brooklyn, who also grew up in a single parent home. Not only do I relate to where he has come from but I also relate to many of his spiritual beliefs.

For many years Jay-Z has been accused of not believing in God or being part of a devil worshiping cult. In an interview with Angie Martinez, he addresses these rumors once and for all and says, "For the record, I of course believe in God, but I believe in one God. If people must know my religious beliefs, I don't believe in religion. I think all that separates people. I think it's one God. I think it's all the same God." While many who practice different religious faiths may not necessarily agree to this I believe that what Jay was conveying was that regardless of what you believe in, there is only one God and whether you call it God, Buddha, Allah, or the Universe, it is all the same.

I recently wrote a book called Mind Right, Life Right: Manifesting dreams through the laws of the universe, and in the book, I discuss 9 mindset principles that anyone can use to get all that they deserve out of life but it first starts with knowledge of self. Not knowledge of all things but knowledge of who you are divinely and why you were put on this earth. Jay has been a champion of this message for some time now. "I'm clear why I'm here! How bout you?" Jay exclaims confidently! But as we seek knowledge of self we must not get too caught up in rules of what we should or should not be doing.

Everybody can tell you how to do it, they never did it! (Jay Voice). Knowledge is a tricky thing; Erykah Badu once eloquently stated, "The man that knows something knows that he knows nothing at all." Which means that the more you seek out knowledge, the more you'll realize that the knowledge you currently have is nothing compared to all of the information and wisdom that is out there in the world. To add to that, in 1 Corinthians 8:2, "Those who think they know something, do not yet know as they ought to know." Or as Socrates puts it "A man who knows he knows nothing is smarter than a man who thinks he knows something but really knows nothing." This simply means that a true quest for knowledge is a never-ending quest. There are no absolutes in the world, so to any conclusion that you may come up with, there will always be more information that either supports that conclusion, contradicts that conclusion, or makes that conclusion seem completely ridiculous.

That's why there is so much separation in the world. Whether it's between religion and science, spirituality and the Bible, the Koran and the Tao Te Ching, The Old Testament vs the New Testament, Christianity vs Judaism vs Buddhism vs Islam vs Bahá'í Faith vs Hinduism or Taoism vs New Age Thinking... most people want certainty. There is a human desire to know what is right or wrong and the need to operate under that structure.

There is also the need to know the outcome of the choices we make in life. Whether heaven or hell is in the afterlife or is it here on earth NOW? Is there truly only one life to live or do we keep coming back until we get it right? Has the outcome of our lives already been predestined or do we have free will to choose as we want? Is there a meaning to life or is this one big Matrix-like virtual simulation?

The answer to these questions are not really known but one thing we know for sure is that life and lessons come to you in stages and as your consciousness increases you'll be ready to accept different truths. For thousands of years, we have been taught how to live by those who came before us. We were told about the consequences of not following the teachings that were left for us to follow. Many interpretations paint a picture of a vengeful and punitive God that will repay us for our wrongdoings. What many fail to realize is that no matter what we believe in, every human being has been given free will by their higher power to do as they wish with their life.

The universe doesn't tell us what we can or can't do, but instead gives us back exactly what we put out to the world through the law of Karma and the Law of Cause and Effect. We are 100% responsible for the consequences of our actions.

Contrary to popular belief the Universe does not aim to punish us. The universe is here to assist us in manifesting whatever we decide to conjure up. If we ask for peace, love and happiness through our thoughts, intentions, and actions then that's what we will experience. If we ask to live in doom and gloom based on what we decide to keep our focus on, then that wish will be ours as well. We decide which direction our life goes. We live in a world that is created for us by us. Give love then get love, spread hate then hate will come back to you, live in fear and fear will be your companion. In fact, for thousands of years, fear has been one of the biggest emotions that has held many back from living the lives that they truly deserve. Release the spirit of fear and live in love; as you live in love you begin to increase your level of consciousness, which will ultimately lead you to your destination.

When Jay says, "This spiritual s#@t really works, he is talking about the ease of manifesting his dreams because he is in tune with his higher self. Keep in mind that the path to your divine self will not be a straight path. Sometimes it's easy to get lost in our physical form but as philosopher Pierre Teilhard de Chardin once said "We are not human beings having a spiritual experience. We are spiritual beings having a human experience." In order to evolve during our human experience, it is necessary that we encounter duality on our journey. This is why we can recognize good and evil, light and darkness, happiness and sadness; these contrasts or "the ying and the yang" as some call it, give us greater perspective and guides us toward our soul's desires. As Curtis Jackson once said "Joy wouldn't feel so good if it wasn't for pain." Knowing what you don't want is just as important as knowing what you do want. Having duality coupled with the right to choose, allows us to act on free will in the world. This gives us the right to be the master of our fate and the co-creator of our world. There is no coincidence that Jay calls himself "Jay Hova, the God MC" He recognizes that God created him (and all of us) in her image, so as God is, so are we. As we recognize our God given powers, we will come to grips with the fact that life is exactly what we make it. This is the Path of Self-realization.

Before we can realize this path or accept this new truth, we must first cleanse ourselves of so many years of misinformation. There are Universal Laws that are working, whether we believe in them or not. The best tangible example of this is the law of gravity. If you throw something in the air it WILL come down. The law of gravity doesn't require your belief system in order to work... it just is! Similarly, the laws of the universe are what they are and are ALWAYS working. Every time we focus on something we are calling it towards us through our super subconscious mind. By using our thoughts and beliefs, we invite the people who are in our lives, the situations that shape our experiences and the material things that add or take away from our human existence. By nature, we have EVERYTHING we need to manifest our dreams and we can do so instinctively but because of the noise in the outside world we often use our energy for resisting what we don't want instead of focusing on what we do want. This process is invoking one of the laws of the universe without us even being aware of it. But are we really unaware? In religion we call it spirits, in science we call it energy, In the streets we call it vibes. All we have to do is trust it.

Our intuition will guide us to go where we need to go but many of us allow logic and the voice of others to drown out what we know instinctively. Some of us think that if we act like something doesn't exist, it will just go away. The truth of the matter is that your dreams will either liberate you or haunt you. Right now, as we speak, you have dreams and aspirations that are calling you and if you don't listen to this calling you will forever live in gloom and doom. Financial abundance is your birthright and if you do not begin to move as though this is fact then your financial freedom will be a steep mountain to climb.

The following 9 principles are important to practice and realize in order to reset your belief system and allow "This spiritual s#@t" to work for you:

#1 - Accept Your Divine Right of Abundance: The Universe is ready and willing to give you EVERYTHING your heart desires. Know and believe that abundance is your Birthright.

#2 - Be Intentional: Your dreams will begin to manifest when you become intentional with your thoughts, feelings, and actions. The Universe responds better to purposeful intentions.

#3 - ALWAYS look on the bright side: The Universe will ALWAYS give you what you put your focus on! Change your perspective and see the good in ALL situations.

#4 - Accept What Is and Change What You Can: What you resist will persist. Never fight against the undesirable. Change what's in your power to change and accept what you cannot.

#5 - Only Take Action That Supports Your Desires: Every action has an equal or greater reaction; therefore, it is

#6 - Embrace Your Struggles: Adversity exist only to strengthen where you are weak. When you successfully overcome obstacles, you are signaling to the universe that you are ready for the next level of life.

#7 - Understand the Power of Collaboration: No two like-minds can come together without creating a third and more powerful like-mind. Use the power of collaboration to manifest your dreams faster.

#8 - Give What You Want to Get Back: You will undoubtedly reap what you sow. Only put out in the world that in which you are willing to get back and that which will lead you towards your desires.

#9 - Allow Your Desires to Come to Fruition: You must have unwavering faith in the abundance of the universe and know without a shadow of a doubt that ALL of your desires WILL become reality in divine time.

Emory Passed You Ninjas and He Did a Bid

"Identity is a prison you can never escape, but the way to redeem your past is not to run from it, but to try to understand it, and use it as a foundation to grow."

- JAY Z

The story of Emory Jones is an inspirational one. Emory "Vegas" Jones is one of Jay-Z's closest friends and his ex-drug-dealing partner. Back in 2000, Emory was convicted of trafficking cocaine and was sentence to 16 years. Allegedly, Emory ran a coke ring in Maryland's Eastern Shore. His arrest came at the height of Jay-Z's career, right when Jay was going to start the Hard Knock Life Tour. We were first introduced to Emory on the Kanye West produced, John Legend featured track "Do You Wanna Ride" off the Kingdome Come album. Basically, the song was an ode to Emory's loyalty to Jay and for standing tall when the heat came down. When the Federalis tried to build a cell around Jay, they snatched Emory up and tried to get him to tell. But he told 12, "Give him 12," He told them to go to hell (I'm paraphrasing Jay-Z's lyrics from Drug Dealers Anonymous).

Emory was released from prison in 2010 and it is said that Jay wrote a letter to the judge during Emory's parole hearing explaining that upon Emory's release, Jay would give him a

$50k job to work as an executive assistant at Roc Apparel Group. With the help of this letter Emory was released early. Emory is now the creative director of Jay's Roc Nation company. In his role, he oversees everything related to apparel. The Roc Nation logo was actually designed by Emory and Jay - which is a paper plane hence why Jay said "Emory Passed You Ninjas and He Did a Bid." Also, the brag that Emory is ahead stems from the facts that since he's been home he has been able to do some major things in the fashion world in a short amount of time.

Emory is also the creative mind behind the "Bet on Yourself" campaign which uses Emory as an example that you are your greatest asset and investing in your talent is necessary for success. The gist is this: No matter what obstacles come your way, no matter what setbacks may try to stop you, you can always get back on top. This is an important lesson as we journey through life and with our finances because as adversity hits, you can either accept defeat or realize that "a loss aint a loss, it's a lesson." With the proper perspective, you can practically overcome anything that life throws at you.

If you were to follow Emory on Instagram (@Vegas_Jones) you will immediately see that no matter what, he always has a positive mental attitude. In fact, I can almost guarantee that this attitude is what helped him get through his bid in prison and what has helped him to take his life back to the top after his release. The importance of having a positive mental attitude can be summed up in three words: Law of Attraction!

For years people have studied this law, coming to the conclusion that a person's thoughts, emotions, and beliefs attract their experience; or simply "you get what you think about most". In my lifetime, I've read plenty of books that focus on the law of attraction which include Think and Grow Rich, The Secret, As a man thinketh, Mr. Everit's Secret and many others. Understanding the law of attraction is a very important step in creating financial freedom; even though a lot of us don't truly recognize its power.

If you take a moment and think, you will realize that your attitude towards something is the reason, whether good or bad, why you are in a particular situation. Think back to anything you've accomplished in your life, I guarantee that at that moment you were in the right frame of mind which in turn attracted it to you. Think about all the things you didn't get, I can also guarantee that in some way you were thinking negatively which in turn created that reality as well. When I say negatively, it can mean different things. Worry, anxiety, stress, fear, etc.; are all negative feelings that will not create wealth nor will it help you obtain any goal or aspiration. There is a saying "the rich get richer and the poor stay poor", most of this has to do with their attitudes. Rich people are rich because they know what it is to live life abundantly, so the fear of not having isn't immediately present. The absence of this fear allows rich people to concentrate on accumulating more wealth, hence the term the rich get richer. On the other hand, the poor only know being poor, so any talk about no longer having to struggle is not reality to them. Because of this, they concentrate on just sustaining life, they live life as it comes and don't have a real expectation of living life abundantly. The poor have an attitude of expecting the worst and hoping for the best. This expectation of the worst is what prolongs misfortune and guarantees that their situation stays constant. Obtaining financial freedom is simple: If you want to change your life you have to change your mind! This has worked for Emory and has absolutely worked for Jay.

As Emory alluded to, the key to success is for you to bet on yourself. You must have unwavering belief in yourself and your ability and do what your heart desires because there are no ceilings! Your circumstance does not define you; its how you respond to them that make the difference. You can either be happy or be miserable.... The work is all the same! Staying in good spirits is vital because what you resist will persist and what you focus on will continue to be part of your reality.

In order to begin to attract the life that you deserve you must first think positively and recondition your mind. Your thoughts create your reality so without changing your mind it will be difficult to change your life. Contrary to popular belief life is easy and most of the things that fear teaches us to worry about hardly ever do happen. Those who try too hard never really obtain true riches and financial freedom. Their eagerness to be successful transcends into anxiety, impatience and fear which are all negative feelings that can never bring abundance. Practicing the following steps will ensure that you look at life the way you were supposed to and begin the process of financial freedom.

1) Improve Your Surroundings:

You must immediately rid yourself of anything in your life that is negative. This includes the type of movies you watch, music you listen to, and people you interact with on a daily basis. As a general rule: If it doesn't make you feel good, you shouldn't be doing it!

Action: Create a list of things that make you feel good. For example; a walk in the park, playing your favorite sport, spending time with your loved ones, etc.; after you have compiled your list, include at least one of these activities in your weekly schedule. If your schedule permits do more than one but one item is the minimum.

2) Be Grateful

Gratitude is one of the best ways to keep a positive attitude. A negative attitude can stem from greed, self-pity, jealousy and not being fully satisfied with what you have now. If you get into the "attitude of gratitude" you will immediately rid yourself of most negative thoughts because you will realize that the things you need in life are already yours. When you're grateful, you begin to think about the less fortunate and realize how you don't really have it that bad. People complain about not having enough money to buy new shoes but what about those folks who have no feet!! You may have thought I was going to say "no shoes" but I took it a step further to show how being grateful to have feet has now diminished the importance of a new pair of shoes. Be grateful for the little things and the bigger things will come easily. Give thanks that you woke up this morning, give thanks that you have the capacity to do what you need to, to change your life and give thanks that you are you.

Action: Create a gratitude list which includes all of the things that you are grateful for. Things we often take for granted like family, friends, employment, shelter, clothes, neighbors, education, food, health, freedom, etc.; as you go through your day remind yourself as often as needed what you are grateful for. Make it a habit to give thanks every morning before you leave the house.

3) Look at the bigger picture

Often times we allow the small things that go wrong to take precedence over the more important things. You must keep your goal in your mind's eye, so the small things won't have such a big effect on your ultimate goal. I had a teacher who once told me, "Don't lose the forest, for the tree". At first, I didn't understand the significance of that statement but now I realize that, that was the best advice someone has ever given me. When you concentrate so much on the small things and give so much negative energy towards it, you jeopardize losing it all and sacrificing all that you have worked hard for.

4) Create Positive Self-Talk

Creating positive self-talk is the process of eliminating yourself of negative thoughts. Words like I can't, I'll try, I hope, I wish, are all defeating words that need to be removed from your vocabulary immediately. Self-Confidence is having full faith in your abilities no matter what and knowing that anything is possible. You must begin the process of telling yourself positive things enough times that it will eventually seep into your subconscious. This method is what most people know as autosuggestion. When you begin to tell yourself positive things, you begin to get rid of all of the negative things that were in your mind and create a positive reality. Lack of confidence is a disease and you must talk to yourself in a positive way and convince yourself that you can become the person that you want to be. Negatively, it is known that if you tell a lie long enough you begin to start to believe that lie. Creating positive self-talk is using that theory positively in order to build self-confidence.

Action: Repeat the following affirmations to yourself every night before you go to sleep

I know that what I think about the most whether positive or negative will eventually come true, so I will think of myself positively and concentrate all of my thoughts daily on the person I want to be and lifestyle I want to live.

I deserve to be happy and successful and now have committed myself, my thoughts and my actions towards this goal and will do whatever it takes to make it so.

I know that I have what it takes to achieve my long and short-term goals. Nothing can stop me! I will stop making excuses and use any obstacles as the fuel I need to keep going.

I have the power to change myself. I will no longer blame others for my circumstances. I will do whatever it takes to turn all of my dreams into reality.

I have full faith in my abilities and trust that by doing my best; I can accomplish any task, no matter how big or small. Impossible is nothing! I vow to do my best in everything I do and will never stop trying until I achieve it.

I know that no type of wealth, money or position will last long if it's not gained through truth and justice. I promise to never indulge in any schemes, scams, cons or any sort of business deal that does not have a positive effect on everyone involved.

By repeating these affirmations every day, I will attract good people and circumstances to bring me closer to my goal. I will eliminate all negative thoughts and feelings. I will no longer feel hatred, envy, jealousy, or selfishness towards anyone. I know that to help others is to help myself, so I will also be of assistance to others and help them in the pursuit of their goals.

5) FAITH IT TIL YOU MAKE IT

Lack of confidence usually stem from self-doubt. Most people give themselves less credit then they deserve by allowing other people's experiences and failures to dictate what they are capable of doing. Faith it til you make it, is the last step in building self-confidence and will give you the courage you need to fully become who you want to be. For so long we were told by friends, family, and society what we can and can't do that we began to believe these limitations. Our belief in these restrictions caused us to doubt many things that we were ready for and capable of doing. "Faith it til you make it" which simply means to become the person you want to be well before you have obtained the status, is the process of proving to yourself that those "limitations" are nonexistent and confirms the FACT that thoughts become things. It is no coincidence that the people who are prosperous in life are the ones who take initiative, do more than they are paid to do, and vividly keep their success in their mind's eye. "Faith it til you make it, is simply giving you the power to do the same!

Action: Create a personal statement of what your ultimate goal in life is. Write down every single detail of what you would like to accomplish, and then write it as if you have attained it already.

For example, My Personal Statement goes as such:

I am happy that I am financially free. I have gained my wealth in various amounts and in various ways.

I am a bestselling author who has written several books that have sold millions of copies. I have sold these copies by providing the best possible book that help and empower anyone who reads it.

I am a film producer who created video series that helped shed light on social and financial issues that have been seen millions of times.

I am a highly sought after paid speaker who receives thousands of dollars per talk. People come and hear me speak over and over, each time touching their hearts and moving them into action.

I am an Emmy Award-winning Talk Show host as well as a Radio personality on a nationally syndicated show. Collectively both shows attract millions of viewers and listeners and have created a dialogue for Self-Improvement.

I created motivational albums that have sold millions of copies via compact disc, mp3's and all other forms of digital format.

I am successful and still have time to spend with my family. I have a perfect work/life balance and a beautiful relationship with my wife and kids. My family and friends are proud of me and I help each of them fulfill their dreams.

All of my ventures provide jobs and entrepreneurial opportunities for all of the people I care for.

I believe in myself and in my abilities, with no restrictions and will continue to live life to its fullest.

As per the example above, your personal statement must be specific and include your definite purpose in life. You must list how you expect to obtain it and what you intend to give back. Begin at once to become the person you want to be; you must walk like it, talk like it, breathe like it, dress like it, think like it. Become It!! Every morning when you wake up, you must repeat your personal statement aloud while looking in the mirror and again before you go to sleep. As you go out into the world remember who that person is and begin to be that person immediately. As time goes on you will subconsciously begin to visualize yourself being that person and as a person thinketh so shall they be!

WARNING! What isn't "Faith it til you make it"? Some people pretend to live a lifestyle that they cannot afford. They don't have their priorities in order and spend money trying to impress others. Playing pretend forces one to have to keep up an image that is not really them; this requires too much energy, wastes money, and doesn't help begin the habit of accumulation. "Faith it til you make it' should only be used in conjunction with your personal statement. Any other use will be counter-productive to financial freedom.

CHAPTER 9:15

What's Better Than One Billionaire... Two!

"I'd rather die enormous than live dormant, that's how we on it."

- JAY Z

Now by this point we have discussed why financial freedom is our only hope, how important it is to forfeit the v12 engine, and why you should make money work for you instead of you working for it. We discussed credit and how "they did it." We gave a step by step guide on the home ownership process, starting a business the right way and how to make "this spiritual s#@t" work, we discussed overcoming adversity and how to "merily, merily, eat off of streams; now it's time to put it all together to build up our community.

There is an African proverb that states "If you want to go fast, go alone. If you want to go far, go together." When Beyoncé told us to get into formation, she was onto something and was giving us the keys to economic freedom for our community. Sometimes we can find inspiration in unlikely places. For instance, Geese know about getting into formation very well. As each goose flaps its wings, it creates an 'uplift' for the birds that follow. By flying in a "V" formation, the whole flock adds about 71% greater flying range than if each bird flew alone. When a goose falls out of formation, it suddenly feels the drag and resistance of flying alone. It quickly moves back into formation to take advantage of the lifting power of the bird immediately in front of it. When the lead goose gets tired, it rotates back into the formation and another goose flies to the point position. The geese flying in formation honk to encourage those up front to keep going! When a goose gets sick, wounded or shot down, two geese drop out of formation and follow it down to help protect it. They stay with it until it dies or is able to fly again. Then, they launch out with another formation of geese and try to catch up with the flock.

There are multiple lessons that can be learned by the way geese move to accomplish their goals.

1. Geese show us that if you connect with people who share a common goal and sense of direction, you can get where you are going quicker and easier because you are traveling on the collective power of one another.

2. Success leaves clues; If you are with a group that is vibrating on your same wavelength then it is in your best interest to follow the lead.

3. When you share resources, knowledge, life experiences, and take turns sharing leadership, then you can accomplish way more together than you could ever accomplish alone.

4. We need to make sure that we are part of a positive and encouraging group that helps motivate each other to keep pushing forward towards our dreams. Where there is encouragement, there is a greater likelihood of the attainment of ALL dreams and aspirations.

5. A group that is truly on the same wave will understand that not all days are alike and that there will be times that extra support is needed. The group will stand by each other... **Not just in good times, that's that sucka s#@%, but in all times, it's just what it is.**

If we take it back to spirituality for a second, this is what we call the Law of Collaboration or The Power of the Mastermind. When two or more people of similar vibration are gathered for a shared purpose, their combined energy, when focused on that purpose is doubled, tripled, quadrupled or more. This concept of the Mastermind alliance has been around for years and has been used by everyone from ancient Kings and Queens to Hip-Hop artist and entertainers.

There is no coincidence that in this modern era all of the hip-hop elites are connected to each other in one shape form or fashion. In fact, if you look at the Roc Nation roster, a mastermind alliance is exactly what is being built aka "A society within society." Since its founding in 2008, Roc Nation has grown into the world's preeminent entertainment company. They work in every aspect of modern entertainment—with recording artists and producers, songwriters, radio and tv personalities and athletes. Their client list includes some of the world's most recognizable names: from Jay-Z, DJ Khaled, Rihanna, Shakira, J. Cole, and Big Sean to Angie Martinez, Van Jones, Yoenis Cespedes, Kevin Durant, Dez Bryant, and Robinson Cano; to name a few. They are a full-service organization, supporting their diverse roster of talent via artist management, music publishing, touring, production, strategic brand development and beyond. They've forged strong partnerships with the world's leading experts in artist management, technology, fashion, and philanthropy, and they are truly redefining the business of entertainment. Even when you look at their extended family, like Bad Boy (Puff, R.I.P. Biggie Smalls), MMG (Rick Ross), Grand Hustle (T.I.) or Ruff Ryders (Swizz Beatz, DMX, The Lox, Etc) you will notice how the power of collaboration has helped propel many of their careers.

When Jay asked, **"What's better than one billionaire?"** he was pointing out that even though he is in a competitive race to being the first Hip-Hop billionaire, he is still supporting his brother Puff in reaching that same milestone. In fact, Forbes recently named Diddy, "Hip Hop's Wealthiest Artist" with a net worth of $820 million, while Jay-Z came in at number two with a net worth of $810 million. Contrary to popular belief, we all don't hate on each other. People say black people hold each other back like crabs in a barrel, conveniently neglecting the fact that the crab's natural habitat is not a barrel. Who built the barrel and who put the crabs inside? Divide and conquer is a real thing. When scarcity is created it makes people think that someone else's victory will result in their lose. They believe in win-lose instead of win-win. They try to stop their competition by any means necessary but as you get truly enlightened you will realize that the more you help others, the more you are helping yourself... **Especially, If they're from the same hue as you!** This notion of "There can only be one," stems back to the times where we weren't in control so we allowed other people to dictate what will and can happen within our culture.

The reason why, Jay will **be damned if he drinks some Belvedere while Puff got CÎROC**, is because as a spirit's owner himself, he understands the power of the collective dollar and how it truly affects our community and our ability to move our culture forward. The more we spend with businesses that employ and support our community, the more powerful we will be as a collective cohesive unit. And before anyone tries to fact check and tell me that Puff doesn't own CÎROC, let me beat you to the punch... CÎROC is owned by the liquor company Diageo, but Puff does have a brand ambassador deal, getting 50% of proceeds from the company (Which constitutes a form of ownership, at least in my mind). Before Diddy signed the deal in 2007, CÎROC was only selling about 60,000 cases per year. For the year of 2009, that number rose to 400,000. As of 2016, CÎROC recorded volume sales of 2.4 million cases. You can try to do the math but it's obvious that with a 50% profit share, we now understand why Puff is bringing in double-digit millions per year, with CÎROC being the bulk of the income.

So Y'all still drinkin' Perrier-Jouët? I guess I ain't get through to you yet, huh! So, let me take it a step further: Throughout Jay-Z's career he has been known to help boost the sales of brands he was fond of by rapping about them in his songs. Cristal is a champagne that Jay undoubtedly made famous, at least among the hip-hop world. Well in 2006, it seemed as if Cristal wasn't grateful for the attention and wanted it to stop. After the managing director of the company that makes Cristal said some racist remarks about rappers promoting their champagne, Jay-Z went on record to say, "It has come to my attention that the managing director of Cristal, Frédéric Rouzaud, views the "hip-hop" culture as "unwelcome attention, I view his comments as racist and will no longer support any of his products through any of my various brands, including the 40/40 Club, nor in my personal life." This boycott of Cristal led to Jay promoting the Perrier-Jouët brand of champagne at his nightclubs, which is a primarily white-owned company. Once Jay saw the success that he was bringing to Perrier-Jouët, he decided that he no longer would be a spectator in the champagne game but instead become a player.

"F**k a piece of the pie, I want the whole cake. "In 2014, Jay bought the Armand de Brignac champagne brand, better known as "Ace of Spades." At the time of his purchase Armand de Brignac had consistently beat out Perrier-Jouët in sales until early 2016 when it trailed behind by a margin of nearly a thousand. Ace of Spades' total numbers have continued to decline since, which speaks to what Jay was trying to convey when he asks "y'all still drinking Perrier Jouet?" in Family Feud. As we speak, Perrier-Jouët is being sold as the champagne of choice in many hip-hop clubs hence his frustration that his own people aren't supporting "Ace of Spades."

So, if you think Jay was only promoting his **100% Black-owned champagne** or the race to a billion, you would be half right; he is promoting that everyone within the culture should support each other in order for us to succeed both individually and collectively. He is promoting unity, self-determination, collective work, responsibility for our own culture, and cooperative economics. If we just had faith in ourselves and realize that our purpose is to come together, the quality of all of our lives would be better. So, if you see your brother or sister struggling, help them out! If you see them succeeding, help them out! That is the mindset that will push us forward.

Despite some progress, the current reality is that African-Americans are the only group in America who do not have a true community. Yes, we have residential neighborhoods but without a commitment to that neighborhood or a real political or economic power structure, we will continue to be at the mercy of others. African-Americans spend approximately 93 percent of their annual disposable income with people who live outside of their neighborhood but this wasn't always the case.

No one could have imagined that the passing of the Civil Rights Act of 1964 – which outlawed racial segregation – would result in African-Americans fleeing and integrating into white suburbs and causing the decline of black communities across America. Before integration in the 1960's, blacks had no choice but to stick together. Black Wall Street in Tulsa Oklahoma was a prime example. The community had 600 businesses, 21 churches, 21 restaurants, 30 grocery stores, 2 movie theatres, 6 private airplanes, plus a hospital, a bank, a post office, schools, libraries, law offices and even a bus systems. Winston Salem, North Carolina had a black city bus line, Black theatres, Black hotels, and Black restaurants. Rosewood, Florida's Black community had three churches, a school, a large Masonic Hall, turpentine mill, a sugarcane mill, a baseball team and a general store. All of these thriving black communities met their demise because of jealous, lying neighbors and after the Civil Rights Act was passed it seemed as if our attempt to rebuild our communities was no longer a priority.

Because of desegregation, the black middle class was able to live wherever they wanted, so they left the inner-city neighborhoods where they had been safe from the hostile white world and opted for the white suburbs. Instead of creating and maintaining our own tables, we were satisfied with a seat at someone else' table and for many we still fight to maintain that seat. This is why many of our black inner-city neighborhoods are now being re-gentrified; because we didn't appreciate what we had when we had it. It is even rumored that the real reason Martin Luther King Jr. was assassinated was because he realized that his fight for civil rights was misguided and instead he started fighting for silver rights (economic equality). He actually addresses this in his book "Where do we go from here."

Building Black communities isn't about segregation from other ethnicities and races, it's about being able to build an infrastructure that is self-reliant and self-sustainable so that first and foremost we are not at the mercy of anyone else and secondly, we now come to the table with power and are in a better position to contribute to the world at large. If we take a page out of the Jewish community's book, we will understand the truth behind, "together we stand, divided we fall." The idea that Jews are good with money is one of the oldest Jewish stereotypes, but it's undeniable that Jews are well-represented in finance and business and have a great deal of power over their own community. The fact that for centuries, Jews were excluded from professional guilds (an association of artisans or merchants who oversee the practice of their craft in a particular town) and denied the right to own land, forced them to work as merchants (early entrepreneurs) and financiers (banks' lending money to entrepreneurs). It also taught them the value of owning land and the importance of business ownership in their community.

I shouldn't have to say this but for clarity Pro-Black isn't Anti-White or Anti-American. Pro-Black is what will allow us to become interdependent (the dependence of two or more people or things on each other). As Martin Luther King once said, "Injustice for one, is injustice for all," but in the same breath, Jay-Z said it best... **"There's much bigger issues in the world, I know! But I first have to take care of the world I know!"**

Another thing that I must clear up; building a Black community is more than just "buying and banking black," It is a movement that will create an infrastructure where one or a few people can't bring it down. It isn't about looking for the next black leader, it is creating a mode of living that will outlive any person or group. Especially because we have history to show us that just because someone is black doesn't mean that they are above exploiting black people, or that they have our collective best interest at heart. We've seen many examples of Black people in power doing more harm to black people than their non-black counterparts, that's why the movement has to be bigger than any one person or leader.

The following are 15 steps to creating economic empowerment and restoring the black community:

Black Money Move #1 - Support Black businesses

According to the Department of Labor, black businesses are the 2nd highest employer of African Americans after the government. With layoffs and cutbacks happening across the country and growing numbers of city and county governments facing financial meltdowns, the outlook for government workers is not good. These changes in public sector employment could devastate the black middle class and ultimately the black community as a whole and continue to bring us back economically to a state of dependency on social programs that are already hurting and slated for cuts.

In fact, according to a recent Washington Post Article, African Americans are the only racial group in the U.S. still making less than they did in 2000; meaning that every other ethnicity is progressing forward, while we are staying stagnant or falling back. If we are serious about improving our communities and providing jobs, we must strengthen black owned businesses. As it stands, Blacks spend less money in black-owned businesses than other racial and ethnic groups spend in businesses owned by members of their groups, including Hispanics and Asians.

As I stated earlier, it doesn't take 100 percent of buying Black to make a dent in the Black community. "If the middle-class black consumers were to spend a little more with black firms and the mainstream firms that engage those black firms, there would be a creation of almost 1 million jobs that could benefit the black community. That means that instead of only 3 cents of every dollar an African American spends in this country going to black owned businesses, we can be more conscious of where our $1.3 trillion spending power will go and in turn create a self- sustainable, economically viable community.

Action: Before you purchase any items, please ask yourself the following questions:

1 - Can I make it?

2 - Can I trade for it?

3 - Can I buy it wholesale?

4 - Can I buy it retail from a black business or supporter of the black community

List of Black Business Directories:

- Maggies List
  http://www.maggieslist.com/
- We Buy Black
  https://webuyblack.com/
  App also available
- The Buy Black Movement
  https://www.buyblackmovement.com
- Let's Buy Black 365
  http://letsbuyblack365.com/

BlackTradeLines is a mobile application that helps users locate the nearest African American owned businesses, deals, events and activities to them. The app uses both a voice enabled search and a built-in GPS locator to find Black-owned entities within a given proximity.

Black Money Move #2 - Practice the Spider-Web Doctrine

The Spider-Web Doctrine was first introduced by Chika Onyeani in his controversial book Capitalist Nigger. His claim is that, "Despite enormous natural resources, Blacks are economic slaves because they lack the "killer-instinct" and "devil-may-care" attitude of the Caucasian, as well as the "spider web economic mentality" of the Asian." According to Onyeani, by adopting this economic concept Blacks will be able to attract wealth to their communities, and trap it there as a spider traps flies. While I may not agree with everything Onyeani asserts in his book, one thing that is for sure is blacks need to dominate business ownership and management where black people are the majority consumer population. This means that if we are not willing to change our spending habits, we must then own or control what we spend money on so that our dollar circulates more in our community instead of leaving and supporting someone else's community.

Our current spending habits include:

- Tobacco $3.3 billion
- Whiskey, wine, and beer $3 billion
- Non-alcoholic $2.8 billion
- Leisure time spending $3.1 billion
- Toys, games, and pets $3.5 billion
- Telephone services $18.6 billion
- Gifts $10 billion
- Charitable contributions $17.3 billion
- Healthcare $23.6 billion

To be more specific, according to a Nielsen study on black Consumption:

» Blacks are more aggressive consumers of media and they shop more frequently.

» Blacks watch more television (37%), make more shopping trips (eight), purchase more ethnic beauty and grooming products (nine times more), read more financial magazines (28%) and spend more than twice the time at personal hosted websites than any other group.

» Blacks make an average of 156 shopping trips per year, compared with 146 for the total market. Favoring smaller retail outlets, blacks shop more frequently at drug stores, convenience stores, and Dollar stores.

» Beauty supply stores are also popular within the black community, as they typically carry an abundance of ethnic hair and beauty aids reside that cater specifically to the unique needs of black hair textures.

Taking all of this into consideration, we must begin to pool our money together and buy back our blocks. Start small but think big.

Action: Learn how to purchase commercial real estate in your neighborhood and begin working on a business plan that will allow you to open businesses that support the black community's consumption habit. Work with other like-minded people in your community to accelerate this strategy.

Black Money Move #3 - Stop Brain Draining the Community

Brain Drain doesn't only happen in black neighborhoods; it happens everywhere. Simply put, brain draining is when you take the smartest and brightest from a country or community and place them in another country or community usually for better pay or living conditions. Many Fortune 500 companies aka Corporate America and The Government are good at aggressively attracting Black talent from schools and providing them with great pay and fancy titles. In return those Black talents usually upgrade their lifestyle which almost always includes changing their zip code. They are now inundated with their new responsibilities at work and their fancy upscale neighborhood that they almost unintentionally abandon their original community.

When this happens to those who are already living in suburbs, it doesn't really do much harm to the black community but for those who are from the inner city, when a brain drain happens, this significantly impacts those who need their smartest and brightest the most. This means that instead of creating new role models that the inner-city kids can look up to, they only see the drug dealer, scammer, rapper, or athlete as their way out. Instead of realizing that many doctors, lawyers, bankers, Corporate CEO's, ETC; came from similar or worst backgrounds then them, inner-city kids try to survive with this lie that no one understands them.

Action: As you are climbing up out of your current circumstance or if you are from an inner-city neighborhood and have done well for yourself make sure you reach back and become visible in your old community. Ideally, we want our smartest and brightest to stick around in the community but if that's not possible at least make it known that you are from where you are from. As the saying goes, "If you're lucky enough to do well, it's your responsibility to send the elevator back down."

BLACK MONEY MOVE #4 - MONETARILY SUPPORT YOUR CIVIL AND SILVER RIGHTS ORGANIZATIONS

Organizations like the NAACP, National Urban League, Operation Hope, World of Money, National Action Network, and many others have been constantly advocating for policies to create more opportunities for black owned businesses (e.g., increasing access to capital) as well as providing civil rights advocacy and financial literacy to the black community. In order for these organizations to survive and continue to advocate for us, we need to support them with our dollars. Also look into organizations like 100Suits and ThatSuitsYou, who do a lot of reentry work with our brothers and sisters who are just coming home. You can donate used suits or clothing that you no longer want for a young person to use to go on interviews.

Action: Add a civil rights or silver rights organization to your budget and provide recurring donations to them on a consistent basis. This can be as little as $10 per pay period. Also consider volunteering your time to some of these organizations

BLACK MONEY MOVE #5 - BANK AT FINANCIAL INSTITUTIONS THAT SUPPORTS OUR COMMUNITY

Historically, black-owned banks have helped stimulate local black communities and financed customers who were turned away by major banks. In recent years our beloved black-run banks have struggled financially, mostly because they took a bigger hit from the housing crisis than the banking industry at large. In fact, the foreclosure crisis hit Blacks' harder than any other group in America. Blacks' homeownership rate has plummeted nearly 6 percent to 46.2 percent since its peak. That's more than twice that of any other racial or ethnic group, as well as the nation's rate as a whole, which fell only 2.3 percent, according to U.S. Census data.

As a community, Blacks also suffered higher-than-average job losses due to the financial crisis which also ultimately hurt black banks. Banking Black is important but what is more important is to make sure the financial institution that you choose to bank with actually lends and supports your community. Don't just bank with a financial institution because of the ownership structure.

If that were the case I would suggest transacting your financial business at a credit union, which is a financial cooperative, and which often are better at providing loans and other financial services cheaply to their members because the members own the institution.

Some churches have credit unions. If you don't have one in your neighborhood think of organizing one, or asking an existing credit union to open a branch in your neighborhood. Usually you only need $5 to open an account.

Also, the importance of having financial institutions that support our community is to provide access to capital for small businesses in order for us to continue to thrive as a community.

Action: Find a financial institution that supports the black community; Preferably a Black bank or Credit Union but if there is a traditional bank, regional bank, or digital bank that can show a record of providing loans and access to capital to your community then that may suffice. Open an account with this financial institution and begin to transition from where you bank now. If you don't have a bank account make sure you begin to take steps towards being banked. If your lack of bank account is due to credit issues then begin rectifying your situation as soon as possible so that you don't waste money unnecessarily and so your money can count towards the upliftment of our community. You are literally throwing money away if you frequent check cashing stores and/or payday lenders.

Black Money Move #6 - Organize a Buying Club

Deli's, Bodega's, and corner grocery stores are literally stiffening billions of dollars from the black community every year. Instead of giving money away in the name of convenience, organize a buying club in your neighborhood, housing co-op or apartment building. Everyday items like toilet paper, paper towels, oil, rice, pasta, flour, sugar, laundry detergent, and seasoning can be purchased in bulk and the cost shared so that everyone gets these items cheaper than what they would pay buying them retail.

Action: Organize a group in your neighborhood or building, elect someone to be in charge of collecting money and purchasing items, make a list of essentials that are needed on a bi-weekly basis, divide cost based on need, visit a wholesale shopping club like Costco's, Sam's club, or Bj's and purchase your items. Rotate responsibility of collecting money and buying every three months.

BLACK MONEY MOVE #7 - START A LENDING CLUB

Insufficient credit history, low credit scores, and lack of access to capital are some reasons why it may be difficult to obtain loans from a bank. Not having access to money during emergencies leads to our community using predatory lending services like Pawn Shops, Payday lenders, title loans, rent-a-centers, etc.; that according to Debt.org cost borrowers $2.1 billion in interest and fees. Borrowers often end up paying $450 in interest alone for a $350 principal because of loan churning. It is commonplace among predatory lenders and something consumers with a poor credit history should be on guard against.

Action: Get a group of 5-7 people together to start to put money together to loan each other money. Five people contributing $50 or $100 could result in a $250 or $500 loan for each member. This method is practiced around the world in places like Africa, Asia and the Caribbean and is known as "susu", and by other names.

BLACK MONEY MOVE #8 -CREATE A COMMUNITY CHILDCARE NETWORK

Lack of childcare can be a real barrier for many in the community who are looking to achieve personal goals. Creating a Community Childcare Network or a Childcare cooperative as it is commonly called can make it more convenient for people to work, go to school, volunteer, or to participate in community organizing.

Childcare cooperatives can start as simple casual babysitting exchanges and can go all the way to highly organized preschools with hundreds of participating families.

Childcare centers usually require operators to obtain licenses from the state where they are operating. However, in many states, there are laws allowing groups to care for their children through a cooperative arrangement, without getting a family child care home license as long as the cooperative arrangement doesn't involve payment and it has to meet all of the following conditions:

» Parents must combine their efforts so that each parent, or set of parents, rotates as the responsible caregiver with respect to all the children in the cooperative.

» Any person caring for the children must be a parent, legal guardian, stepparent, grandparent, aunt, uncle, or adult sibling of at least one of the children in the cooperative.

» There can be no payment of money or receipt of in-kind income in exchange for care. This does not prohibit in-kind contributions of snacks, games, toys, blankets for napping, pillows, and other materials parents deem appropriate for their children. This does not prohibit payment for outside activities, like park admission fees, but the amount of that payment may not exceed the actual cost of the activity.

» No more than 12 children can receive care in the same place at the same time.

Action: Survey your apartment, housing co-op, street or subdivision to see who would be interested in a childcare cooperative. Google "(Insert Your State) childcare license" to learn whether or not you need a license to operate and what rules govern your particular area.

Black Money Move #9 - Unify Your Neighborhood

Once upon a time and not very long ago, it took a village to raise not only the child but the village itself. There were support systems in place and everyone looked after each other. Now in days we barely make eye contact with our neighbors. It's time to unify our neighborhoods in order to build trust and empowerment within our community. This begins with having open dialogue, creating a safe space for people to deal with trials and tribulations, supporting our youth from an educational front, and bridging the gap between our most vulnerable population; the youth and our elders.

Action: Organize a discussion group around local issues, organize support groups such as for single mothers/fathers, formerly incarcerated, those caring for elderly parents, etc. to share ideas and best practices, or to have an outlet for ideas, support and creativity.

Create Enrichments programs for our youth where we enrich and support students who demonstrate advanced reading and/or math abilities for their age. Also form Peer-to-peer tutor groups for those who may be falling behind but can be lent a hand by their counterparts in school

Bridge the Gap Between Youth & Elders. Carry bags, rake leaves or shovel snow for elderly people and trade them for a cooked meal, childcare, cooking lessons, or some other knowledge trade. Talk to an elder in your neighborhood and learn some of the ways that they survived hard times. Share the knowledge.

Black Money Move #10 - Start a Community Garden

Many parts of our community are considered Food deserts because of the lack of healthy and fresh foods. As per the USDA; Food deserts are defined as parts of the country that are lacking fresh fruit, vegetables, and other healthful whole foods, usually found in impoverished areas. This is largely due to a lack of grocery stores, farmers' markets, and healthy food providers. Health is wealth! We cannot have an economically viable community if we are not living long enough to contribute to it long term. Here are some alarming health statistics for African Americans:

- Diabetes is 60% more common in black Americans than in white Americans. Blacks are up to 2.5 times more likely to suffer a limb amputation and up to 5.6 times more likely to suffer kidney disease than other people with diabetes.

- African-Americans are three times more likely to die of asthma than white Americans.

- Strokes kill 4 times more 35- to 54-year-old black Americans than white Americans. Blacks have nearly twice the first-time stroke risk of whites.

- Blacks develop high blood pressure earlier in life -- and with much higher blood pressure levels -- than whites. Nearly 42% of black men and more than 45% of black women aged 20 and older have high blood pressure.

- Cancer treatment is equally successful for all races. Yet black men have a 40% higher cancer death rate than white men. African-American women have a 20% higher cancer death rate than white women.

And why do these health disparities exist? According to Clyde W. Yancy, MD, associate dean of clinical affairs and medical director for heart failure and transplantation at the University of Texas Southwestern Medical Center, genes definitely play a role but so does the environment in which people live, socioeconomic status and, yes, racism. The fact that many of our communities don't have many healthy options are cause for a lot of our health issues.

Action: There are many black farmers struggling to sell their produce. Seek them out or buy a share in a Community

Supported Agriculture program which is a program that allows city residents to have direct access to high quality, fresh produce grown locally by regional farmers. You can also join with other community gardeners in existing gardens or shop at a farmers' markets. If all else fails, the following steps are adapted from the American Community Garden Association's guidelines for launching a successful community garden in your neighborhood:

1. Organize a Meeting of Interested People

Determine whether a garden is really needed and wanted, what kind it should be (vegetable or organic?), whom it will involve and who benefits. Invite neighbors, tenants, community organizations, gardening and horticultural societies, building superintendents (if it is at an apartment building)—in other words, anyone who is likely to be interested.

2. Form a Planning Committee

This group can be comprised of people who feel committed to the creation of the garden and have the time to devote to it, at least at this initial stage. Choose well-organized persons as garden coordinators Form committees to tackle specific tasks: funding and partnerships, youth activities, construction and communication.

3. Identify All Your Resources

Do a community asset assessment. What skills and resources already exist in the community that can aid in the garden's creation? Contact local municipal planners about possible sites, as well as horticultural societies and other local sources of information and assistance. Look within your community for people with experience in landscaping and gardening.

4. Approach A Sponsor

Some gardens "self-support" through membership dues, but for many, a sponsor is essential for donations of tools, seeds or money. Churches, schools, private businesses or parks and recreation departments are all possible supporters. One garden raised money by selling "square inches" at $5 each to hundreds of sponsors.

5. Choose A Site

Consider the amount of daily sunshine (vegetables need at least six hours a day), availability of water, and soil testing for possible pollutants. Find out who owns the land. Can the gardeners get a lease agreement for at least three years? Will public liability insurance be necessary?

6. Prepare and Develop the Site

In most cases, the land will need considerable preparation for planting. Organize volunteer work crews to clean it, gather materials and decide on the design and plot arrangement.

7. Organize the Garden

Members must decide how many plots are available and how they will be assigned. Allow space for storing tools, making compost and don't forget the pathways between plots! Plant flowers or shrubs around the garden's edges to promote good will with non-gardening neighbors, passersby and municipal authorities.

8. Plan for Children

Consider creating a special garden just for kids–including them is essential. Children are not as interested in the size of the harvest but rather in the process of gardening. A separate area set aside for them allows them to explore the garden at their own speed.

9. Determine Rules and Put Them in Writing

The gardeners themselves devise the best ground rules. We are more willing to comply with rules that we have had a hand in creating. Ground rules help gardeners to know what is expected of them. Think of it as a code of behavior. Some examples of issues that are best dealt with by agreed upon rules are: dues, how will the money be used? How are plots assigned? Will gardeners share tools, meet regularly, handle basic maintenance?

10. Help Members Keep in Touch with Each Other

Good communication ensures a strong community garden with active participation by all. Some ways to do this are: form a telephone tree, create an email list; install a rainproof bulletin board in the garden; have regular celebrations. Community gardens are all about creating and strengthening communities.

BLACK MONEY MOVE #11 - ADOPT A SCHOOL IN YOUR NEIGHBORHOOD

Malcolm X once famously said, "Only a fool would let his enemy teach his children." It is our responsibility to make sure that what we are giving our children the proper guidance they need to excel in the real world. Ideally, we need more of our local men and women to become teachers in our public schools or we need to continue to build our own private and charter schools but we can also contribute to the young community's education by adopting a school in your neighborhood.

Action: Identify a middle school or high school in your neighborhood and volunteer to speak to the students during the school's career day. If the school doesn't have a career day speak with administration to allow you to go in and speak to students on a consistent basis. It can be once a year or one a quarter; just make sure you are visible for the students.

Also, take some time out to teach young people in your community skills such as basic electrical work, carpentry, machine repair, photography, cooking, nursing, etc. This way you help young people gain skills which could result in employment, or even them starting their own business.

Black Money Move #12 - Get Involved with Local Politics

As a community, we focus a lot on the big elections like, President, Governor and Mayor but what we need to realize is that while those political offices are very important, your local government is equally or more important to your everyday life. Your local politicians work for you and your community. When you can control local politics, you can help dictate how certain public funds get spent and what resources are sent to your neighborhood. Would you like to see schools be funded more, or, does your community need a recreation center? Make your desires known to the City Council and you can work hard to help achieve them.

Action: The best way to get involved with local politics is to get out there and get started:

1. Know who your local legislators and politicians are
2. Know how to get in touch with them
3. Attend town hall meetings
4. Attend City Council meetings
5. Get to know your local School Board
6. Join your local PTA
7. Join a voting league or political organization

8. Join a campaign
9. Volunteer at their headquarters
10. Run for office or Raise money for a candidate

Black Money Move #13 - Police Your Own Community

It is no secret that in the history of America, Black and Brown people have had a very strenuous relationship with the police. In fact, recent history has proven to show that some of the fears from the past are still very much alive.

Philando Castile, 32 and black, was fatally shot during a traffic stop in a suburb of St. Paul, Minn; Alton Sterling, 37 and black, was shot twice at point-blank range while pinned to the ground in Baton Rouge, La.; Freddie Gray, 25 and black, suffered a spinal injury while riding in the back of a police transport van in Baltimore. He died a week later; Walter Scott, 50 and black, was fatally shot in the back while running away from a police officer in North Charleston, S.C. Scott was unarmed; Tamir Rice, 12 and black, died a day after being shot by police responding to a call of a juvenile waving a gun inside a Cleveland park. Tamir was holding a toy pellet gun; Laquan McDonald, 17 and black, was shot 16 times while walking in the middle of a Chicago street. He was carrying a knife; Michael Brown, 18 and black, was shot dead during an altercation with a cop in Ferguson, Mo. Brown was unarmed; Eric Garner, 43 and black, died after an NYPD officer put him in a chokehold on Staten Island. Garner, approached by cops for selling loose cigarettes, was unarmed. I can go on but I'm sure you get my point.

It's time to demand change in our neighborhoods so that we are not afraid of cops or criminals. We want our communities to be safe places where we can raise kids and thrive. We can start by community policing, which involves forming partnerships with community organizations, prioritizing transparency, actively pursuing feedback and establishing programs that allow police to engage with residents outside of the law enforcement arena.

The goal is to allow community members to feel heard, respected and empowered to help police control crime in their neighborhoods, rather than feel like police are only there to enforce laws through aggressive stopping, questioning, arresting and throwing people in jail. Community policing means working proactively and building relationships in the face of tension and issues.

Another effective strategy is one employed by many communities that are plagued with violence and it is to create a violence interrupter program. Cure Violence is a Chicago based organization that has created an effective model to "cure violence." The Cure Violence Health Model has been implemented in cities everywhere. In big cities such as New York City, Chicago, Baltimore, San Antonio and New Orleans. In smaller cities like Kansas City, Syracuse and Albany. And all over the world – from San Pedro Sula, Honduras to Cape Town, South Africa.

Action: Any community that has a problem with violence should consider implementing the Cure Violence Health Model. In order to start implementing the Cure Violence health model, someone from the community needs to step up and champion the cause. This can be anyone from the community – a health department, an elected official, a pastor, a community organization or even a concerned citizen.

Whomever initiates the process, the Cure Violence team can help guide you through this process. You can start by visiting http://cureviolence.org/

1. Path to implementing Cure Violence health approach:
2. Assess violence problem and community
3. Engage community leaders
4. Identify appropriate community partners

5. Identify appropriate hospital response partners
6. Re-examine the data
7. Hire and train credible workers
8. Implement program with technical assistance

BLACK MONEY MOVE #14 - GET YOUR MIND AND YOUR BODY RIGHT

Being Black in America isn't always easy. Even our most distinguished face hardships in the name of racism and discrimination. But in order to build our own and coexist on this land we must take care of ourselves physically, mentally and emotionally.

Action: Make sure you are eating well, exercising at least 3 days per week for a minimum of 30 minutes, pray daily, meditate twice a day and commune with other people. Also, be sure to balance your life with "fun." The stronger and well balanced you are, the harder and more creatively you can work to build an enjoyable life for yourself, family, and community.

BLACK MONEY MOVE #15 - PRACTICE SILENCE & GO WITHIN

When chaos happens and doubt starts to seep in, it is important to remember your source. The outside world will continue to try to convince you that you don't have power but remember, "Those who go within, can NEVER do without." Solutions to any problem or obstacle usually spring forth when you take time to unplug out of the Matrix to listen.

Action: Spend time alone every day to meditate, contemplate or listen to the voice of God/The Universe.

CHAPTER 10:26

Generational Wealth, That's the Key

"Leave a mark they can't erase, neither space nor time."

- JAY Z

The culmination of the album and this book are one in the same. Generational Wealth! That's the key! The goal is to start a society within society. Instead of begging and pleading to be accepted by others, we must create our own and break the cycle of poverty. Not just for one or a few but for all. There is no reason why the top 1% control 38.6% of the nation's wealth. Why are the richest 400 Americans wealthier than the entire US black population and 1/3 of the Latino population combined? How do we take the modern-day advances in our economic situations to turn the tides on the wealth gap and economic inequality?

When Jay-Z speaks of generational wealth, he is talking about money and assets that are passed down to future generations. The song Legacy opens with Blu Ivy asking, "Daddy what's a will?" then Jay uses his lyrical skills to explain the importance of preserving the Carter family name and providing his family the tools to build on his wealth for many years to come. It's important to point out here that he also emphasizes that she has to run this hard just to stay in place. This statement is key because 70% of wealthy families lose their wealth by the second generation, and a stunning 90% by the third. According to Chris Heilmann, U.S. Trust's chief fiduciary executive, this is because wealthy families were taught not to talk about money, they worry their children will become lazy and entitled, and they fear the information will leak out. This in turn led to the next generation not being financially responsible enough to handle inheritance, therefore we must teach our children to maintain what we build and not just give them handouts. They must know and be taught what it took to create it and understand that work is required to keep it alive and prosperous. This was always Jay's plan, in a 1999 interview with FLIPSIDE magazine, Jay said, "You know black people don't really inherit businesses that our fathers left for us, so it was to do something like that. That was the big picture right there, for us to build a company that could be passed down to our kids and their kids."

So how does wealth work? There are only three ways to achieve wealth; You either create it from scratch, acquire it through redistribution, or do both. And just for clarity, wealth is making your money work for you; having a large amount of possessions and assets that continue to appreciate over time. You can also create wealth by profiting from someone else's labor. The less someone is paid for their hard work, the more wealth the owner of the business accumulates. This might be obvious but there is no wealth potential in a job, it is the owner who will benefit long term from a worker's long hours. That's why Jay said, "Until you own your own, you can't be free!"

Jay had to start his wealth accumulation from scratch which is evident with the line, "Generational wealth, that's the key, my parents ain't have s**t, so that shift started with me." And the reason why he is giving you $1million worth of game for $9.99 is because he wants the shift to start with you. There are dire consequences when you don't do what needs to be done in order to protect your assets. We've seen this recently with the passing of Prince and the chaos that ensued afterwards trying to figure out where his assets would go.

Before his death, Prince had an exclusive streaming contract with Tidal. In fact, Prince's career goes back over 50 years and in those years, he has had many issues with his label where he felt that he wasn't maintaining creative control of his music. As a result, he broke with his record label, changed his name and yanked his songs off of popular streaming services to prove a point; that no one could tell him what to do with his music. That's why his exclusive Tidal deal was a big deal. It was a win for artist everywhere. Jay-Z explains their agreement in Caught Their Eyes, "I sat down with Prince, eye to eye. He told me his wishes before he died." Prince discussed his decision to exclusively stream his music with Tidal, "After one meeting, it was obvious that Jay Z and the team he has assembled at Tidal recognize and applaud the effort that real musicians put into their craft to achieve the very best they can at this pivotal time in the music industry." Despite what Prince wanted to happen, because he didn't have a will, the estate fought this agreement.

This guy had 'Slave' on his face you think he wanted his masters with his masters? Under a court mandate, the estate had to get the most value from Prince's catalog of about 1,000 songs including "Purple Rain" and "When Doves Cry," hence why the estate challenged the exclusive rights that Tidal had. The argument was that since none of Prince's music was allowed to be on other popular streaming services like iTunes and Spotify, the estate is losing out on a significant part of potential revenue and the courts agreed. Keep in mind that if there was a will in place, then the courts would have no say in this decision. They also had to move fast because under estate law, an estate has nine months after someone's death to determine the value of the estate in order to pay the estate taxes owed. Ultimately the estate was placed under the administration of a Minnesota bank as well as Prince's sister and five half-siblings. The estate would later establish a publishing deal with Universal Music for Prince's catalog.

Subsequently, the estate reopened dialogue with services like Spotify, Apple Music, Amazon Music and iHeart Radio. Before any deals between the streaming services and the estate were officially announced, Spotify not-so-subtly began celebrating the arrival of Prince's music to their service with a series of purple billboards in New York's Union Square subway station. Warner Bros. and NPG Records announced the releases of a remastered version of Purple Rain and the greatest hits collection, Prince 4Ever. The estate also announced an agreement with Universal Music Group to release his music recorded after 1995 alongside music from his vault, including outtakes, demos and live recordings. Again, we ask... You think he wanted his masters with his masters?

The sad part is that Prince's intent is irrelevant because he never wrote it down. That's why it is imperative that people write their intents down. So back to Blu Ivy's question "What's a will?" A will is a document which provides specific instructions regarding the disposition of a person's property and assets after they die. One important note or exception to the rule is that there are other assets such as life insurance, retirement accounts, and jointly owned property that pass to beneficiaries without a will.

When most people hear the words "will," "trust" or "estate planning" they automatically think that these are things reserved for millionaires and billionaires. This couldn't be the furthest thing from the truth; regardless of how much money you have, you must have a plan for what will happen to your assets and who should receive the things you own after you leave this earth.

An estate plan can be something as simple as having life insurance for your family and naming a beneficiary for your retirement accounts, or as complicated as having several trusts for different purposes in addition to your will. Regardless of what direction you decide to go, it is important that you put a transition plan in place to maintain the continuity of your family business that outlives you. Estate planning is more than just having a will. It is a plan that is put in place in order to lessen the financial impact of your death on those you leave behind.

At minimum, estate planning is for the benefit and care of your loved ones, making the legal and financial issues easier to deal with if you pass away. But it is also a tool to transfer wealth and maintain your family legacy. Every competent adult should have a succession plan aka an estate plan especially if you have children. Problems with probate, creditors, con artists, lawsuits, lawyers and death taxes can all delay the settlement of your estate but without a proper plan in place you can really jeopardize your wishes. After Prince's death, more than 45 people came forward as potential heirs to his estate, with many claiming to be a wife, child, sibling or other relative. Even though most were denied, this still complicates payment to the rightful heirs which we still don't know if Prince would've wanted them included in his succession plan. All this to say, estate planning is important.

Prince died without a will so the technical term is known as dying intestate. When this happens, relatives of the deceased have to go through probate court to claim ownership of any assets. We all wish this was a smooth process but more often than not fights between family members happen over who should get what. In this case, the state decides how the deceased's property is passed to their heirs. If no heirs fit the state's formula, the assets may become property of the state meaning they keep your assets and auction them off to cash in on them. A will helps you avoid all of this and simply allows you to control the distribution of your assets and state your final wishes.

One other very important use of a will is that it allows you to recommend a guardian to care for your children or other dependent beneficiaries in the event of your death. When Pop Icon Michael Jackson died he used a will to assign his mother, Katherine Jackson, as the guardian for his three minor children. If Katherine Jackson was unable or unwilling to serve as the children's guardian, then Diana Ross (yes, that Diana Ross) was named to serve as the backup guardian.

Because the responsibility of taking care of a child can be overwhelming, you should select your guardian(s) carefully and get their permission before you list them in your will. Ultimately, the final decision of guardianship will be made by the court, but the courts give a lot of weight to the parent's decision in the will.

You should also name the executor or administrator of your estate and how you would like that person to distribute your assets in your will. This should include how all your debts, taxes and funeral expenses will be paid. A non-contestability clause will help you avoid family disputes. There is also a provision that says, if any beneficiary contests the will, his or her share becomes null and void. Choose using a non-contestability clause wisely, it's not suitable for every family's circumstance.

Now for the fun part... Remember when Jay-Z said he wanted to take his money and spread across his family? Giving a piece to his sisters, Hattie and Lou, the nephews, cousins, TT Eric, and then the rest would go to B for whatever she wants to do? She might start an institute, she might put poor kids through school? Ok, most of that would've went into his will, especially because he is giving his family an option on what they can do with the money. But what if he didn't want to give them a choice and instead he wanted to be sure that even after his death, his money would be spent in the right way? This is where a trust comes into play.

The terms will and trust are often confused but they are very different in a few ways. A will which is actually short for last will and testament only goes into effect after the death of the testator (the person who wrote it). A living trust on the other hand goes into effect as soon as it is signed. You can change both a will and/or trust up until the time of your death as long as you remain mentally competent. The except to this is if you put into effect an irrevocable living trust, which is what the name implies; irrevocable, meaning it will last forever.

A trust is a legal arrangement where one person, called a "settlor" or "grantor," gives assets to another person (or an institution, such as a bank or law firm), called a "trustee." The trustee holds legal title to the assets for another person, called a "beneficiary." A living trust can govern and distribute any property it has been funded with. The person who created the trust, transfers his/her assets into it after it is formed. While any assets that are passed through a will require a probate court, assets in a trust do not require probate. The trust allows for control on how money can be spent because it can hold assets for the benefit of certain beneficiaries, such as minor children who cannot legally take ownership of their own property or any family member you feel would misuse their inheritances. You can literally instruct the trust to only pay a certain amount over a certain period of time to avoid overspending and/or the depletion of moneys.

Wills also become a matter of public record when they're submitted to the court for probate. The terms of living trusts remain private. Again, wills go into effect when you die while Trust can provide for you during life and death. Remember earlier when we discussed Jay-Z and Beyoncé buying a home, well they did so using a blind trust.

Life insurance can also be a great form of asset protection and wealth preservation. Insurance in its simplest terms means "Just in Case". It provides you piece of mind in the form of monetary compensation just in case something happens. Life insurance specifically is an agreement between you and an insurance company which states that in return for your monthly payments they agree to provide any person or persons you choose, called beneficiaries, a lump sum of money in the case of your demise. After someone dies, there are many things that need to be taken care of such as funeral arrangements, taxes, mortgage payments, car loans, credit card debts, and other expenses. The most common use of life insurance is to supplement the loss of income that occurs. When you die and your money stops coming in, besides the grief that comes with the loss, your family may be left with limited resources which cause additional stress and anguish. Life insurance alleviates that and allows life to go on after the death of a loved one.

While most people use life insurance to cover final expenses, it can also be used to cover sending children to college and maintaining your family's lifestyle. The amount of insurance needed depends on a few variables which include your marital status, the size of your family, what expenses you have, what stage of your career you are in and what your goals and aspirations are. There are many types of life insurances and the costs are determined by many factors which include age, sex, and health. Simply put you can purchase life insurance with a death benefit large enough to cover all of the expenses that may come up after death; like estate taxes, mortgages, creditors, etc.;

Action: How to Start on Your Estate Planning:

Now that you understand the importance of having a will, trust, and life insurance, here's a list of steps that gives an overview of the estate planning process:

- Make a list of all your assets and liabilities.

- Purchase life insurance

- Start a family discussion about who should be the guardian for your children.

- Check and update your current beneficiaries on your IRA, 401(K)'s, LIfe Insurance policies, etc;

- Review the current estate tax exemption limits so you'll know how much you can transfer to heirs' tax free.

- Determine how your money will be distributed upon your death (family, charity, etc.).

- Discuss your funeral arrangements with your spouse or family.

- Seek the assistance of a certified estate-planning attorney.

Keep in mind that direct transfers to your spouse are not taxed - these assets are not taxed until s/he dies (this is called a marital deduction).

Below are some Estate-Reduction and Planning Options

- Use trusts to maximize the exclusion and avoid probate. Trusts help you do so because they are designated to a beneficiary.
- Take advantage of charitable donations to reduce your estate.
- Use your estate to pay family educational and medical expenses as these are tax deductible.
- Loan assets to family members to minimize your estate.
- Buy life insurance to help pay estate taxes, but remember life insurance will provide payouts only under certain conditions (executor or beneficiary should be owner).
- Utilize annual gifting to minimize taxes and maximize the value to your loved ones on your will.
- Set up durable powers of attorney.
- Establish your funeral and burial plans.

Make sure you get professional help from your financial advisor, an estate-planning specialist or a lawyer specializing in estates.

Declaration of Financial Independence

I will no longer live rich and die broke. I will spend my money wisely and direct a majority of what I earn towards income producing assets.

I will no longer blow my money trying to look or act rich. I will live below my means while still living life to the fullest.

I will no longer take my credit for granted and instead use it as a tool to leverage and grow my wealth.

I will check my credit score monthly and work on either obtaining or maintaining at 700+ credit score.

I will stop making my landlord rich. I will take the proper steps to become and stay a home owner.

I will forever believe in my ability to create and will use this God-given ability to take chances over advances.

Everything I do is successful. I never lose because I understand that a loss ain't a loss it's a lesson.

I will have unwavering faith in myself and in my higher power. Knowing that I am made in God's likeness, I will move with this knowledge and take what I deserve from life.

I will happily and merrily eat off of multiple streams of income. I will build a financial foundation that cannot be easily broken.

I will stop looking at my brothers and sisters as competition. I will support them and they will support me. I will do everything in my power to create cooperative economics.

I will always keep a proper perspective, knowing that I can overcome any obstacle that comes my way.

I am focused, determined, and committed to building generational wealth for me, my family and community.

I will pass down my knowledge to those around me, knowing that knowledge is one thing I can give away without losing any.

By signing below, I am declaring my divine right to live abundantly. I am certifying and claiming my victory. Nothing can stop me but me!

_____

(Sign Above)

CHAPTER 11:13

About the Author

"I believe excellence is being able to perform at a high level over and over."

- JAY Z

Ash Exantus aka Ash Cash is a 15-year banking executive, personal finance expert, motivational speaker, and the author of two Amazon.com bestselling books (Mind Right, Money Right: 10 Laws of Financial Freedom and What the FICO: 12 Steps to Repairing Your Credit).

He is a business consultant, and spiritual adviser to entrepreneurs, celebrities, athletes, and executives. He is also a Financial teacher as well as a Leadership Council member of the World of Money Financial Institute, a 501(c)(3) non-profit organization whose mission is to empower youth with an immersive financial and technology education, creating financially responsible adults one child at a time.

Ash has established himself as a thought leader and trusted voice with Corporate America, Colleges, Churches, and Community based organizations. Through his message of fiscal responsibility, entrepreneurship, and wealth empowerment, he has become a regular speaker at national conferences across the country. Ash has been featured on popular, national media outlets such as CNN, The New York Times, WSJ, American Banker, CNBC, TheStreet.com, Black Enterprise, Essence Magazine, Ebony, BET, Pix11 Morning News, and countless others.

He is the host of his own radio show titled The Ash Cash Show, which airs live on WHCR 90.3FM NY with a current reach of 2.2 Million listeners. His show is also available via podcast on iTunes, Google Play, iHeartRadio, Spotify, Stitcher and on the TuneIn App

Above all of his credentials, accolades, and titles, Ash is simply known for helping people maximize their full potentials. He thoroughly enjoys his life in Metropolitan New York Area, where he resides with his wife, and two children. You can also read more about Ash by visiting *www.IamAshCash.com*

Made in the USA
San Bernardino, CA
18 January 2018